LABOUR AND VALUE

Labour and Value

Rethinking Marx's Theory of Exploitation

Ernesto Screpanti

https://www.openbookpublishers.com

© 2019 Ernesto Screpanti

This work is licensed under a Creative Commons Attribution 4.0 International license (CC BY 4.0). This license allows you to share, copy, distribute and transmit the work; to adapt the work and to make commercial use of the work providing attribution is made to the author (but not in any way that suggests that they endorse you or your use of the work). Attribution should include the following information:

Ernesto Screpanti, *Labour and Value: Rethinking Marx's Theory of Exploitation*. Cambridge, UK: Open Book Publishers, 2019. https://doi.org/10.11647/OBP.0182

In order to access detailed and updated information on the license, please visit https://www.openbookpublishers.com/product/1066#copyright

Further details about CC BY licenses are available at http://creativecommons.org/licenses/by/4.0/

All external links were active at the time of publication unless otherwise stated and have been archived via the Internet Archive Wayback Machine at https://archive.org/web

Any digital material and resources associated with this volume are available at https://www.openbookpublishers.com/product/1066#resources

Every effort has been made to identify and contact copyright holders and any omission or error will be corrected if notification is made to the publisher.

ISBN Paperback: 978-1-7837-4779-5
ISBN Hardback: 978-1-7837-4780-1
ISBN Digital (PDF): 978-1-7837-4781-8
ISBN Digital ebook (epub): 978-1-7837-4782-5
ISBN Digital ebook (mobi): 978-1-7837-4783-2
DOI: 10.11647/OBP.0182

Cover design by Anna Gatti. Cover image: photo by Zeyn Afuang on Unsplash, https://unsplash.com/photos/9xp0AWvlGC4.

The sphere of circulation or *commodity exchange*, within whose boundaries the sale and purchase of labour-power goes on, is in fact a very Eden of the innate rights of man. It is the exclusive realm of Freedom, Equality, Property and Bentham. Freedom, because both buyer and seller of a commodity, let us say, of labour-power, are determined only by their own free will. They contract as free persons, who are equal before the law. Their contract is the final result in which their joint will finds a common legal expression. Equality, because each enters into relation with the other as with a simple owner of commodity, and they exchange equivalent for equivalent. Property, because each disposes only of what is his own. And Bentham, because each looks only to his own advantage [...]. And precisely for that reason, either in accordance with the pre-established harmony of things, or under the auspices of the omniscient providence, they all work together to their mutual advantage, for the common weal, and in the common interest. When we leave this sphere of simple circulation or the exchange of commodities, which provides the 'free-trader *vulgaris*' with his views, his concepts and the standard by which he judges the society of capital and wage-labour, a certain change takes place, or so it appears, in the physiognomy of our *dramatis personae*. He who was previously the money-owner now strides out in front as a capitalist; the possessor of labour-power follows as his worker. The one smirks self-importantly and is intent on business; the other is timid and holds back, like someone who has brought his own hide to market and now has nothing else to expect but a tanning.

(Marx 1976a, 280)

Contents

Acknowledgments	1
Introduction	3
1. Abstract Labour as a Natural Substance	15
1.1 The Double Abstraction	17
1.2 Labour as a Natural Abstraction	20
1.3 Value Form and Substance	23
1.4 Abstract Labour as a Productive Force	26
2. Abstract Labour as a Historical Reality	31
2.1 The Labour Exchange: From Hegel to Marx	32
2.2 The Subsumption and Subordination of Labour	34
2.3 Abstract Labour as Resulting from a Social Relation	40
3. Labour Subsumption and Exploitation	45
3.1 The Production of Absolute Surplus Value	48
3.2 The Production of Relative Surplus Value	53
3.3 Wage Dynamics	57
4. Values and Prices	63
4.1 Labour Values	65
4.2 Production Prices	67
4.3 The Transformation Problem	70
5. Measures of Exploitation	75
5.1 Two Paradoxes	76
5.2 A Single System Approach	80
5.3 Back to the Real World	85
Conclusions: Rethinking Exploitation	89
Appendix 1. Reproduction Conditions	101
Appendix 2. Advanced or Postponed Wage Payments?	105
References	111

Acknowledgements

This work summarises and re-elaborates ideas I have been developing in several publications and throughout a lengthy research activity. The conciseness and simplicity I have been finally able to achieve is the result of a process of refinement that would have been impossible without the contribution of many friends who provided their encouragement, their suggestions and criticisms. I wish to thank them all, but in particular: Ash Amin, Rakesh Bhandari, Sam Bowles, Paul Cockshott, Matt Cole, Richard Cornwall, Massimo De Angelis, Jim Devine, Emilio Dìaz, Panayotis Economopoulos, David Ellerman, Duncan K. Foley, Argo Golski, Geoff Hodgson, Douglas Koritz, Gerald Levy, Yahya M. Madra, John McDermott, Gary Mongiovi, Edward Nell, Ugo Pagano, Fabio Petri, Angelo Reati, Roberto Renò, Francesco S. Russo, Neri Salvadori, Gilbert L. Skillman, Ian Steedman, Emma Thorley, Marco P. Tucci, Andrew Tylecote, Alberto Valli, Andrea Vaona, Roberto Veneziani, Paul Zarembka and Maurizio Zenezini. I also wish to thank the Association for Economic and Social Analysis and the journal *Rethinking Marxism* for the permission to use materials previously published as 'Karl Marx on Wage Labour: From Natural Abstraction to Formal Subsumption' (Screpanti 2017).

Introduction

There are two alternative approaches to the theory of capitalist exploitation: normative or descriptive. The former aims to prove that capitalism is unjust because it is based on the extraction of surplus value from labour power; the latter seeks to explain the social process through which surplus value is produced.

The normative approach postulates some universal principles of justice so that capitalism may be examined to reveal the illegitimacy of surplus value. Various socialist thinkers, more or less implicitly, assume Locke's axiom of self-ownership. This posits that, by natural law, a free individual is the owner of herself, her talents and abilities, and therefore of the fruits of their use. If another person appropriates these fruits without the consent of the legitimate owner, unjust exploitation occurs.

The Ricardian socialist, Thomas Hodgskin (1825, 83), uses this principle to condemn capitalism. He asserts that "the labour of a man's body and the work of his hands are to be considered as exclusively his own. I take it for granted, therefore, […] that the whole produce of labour ought to belong to the labourer". In a natural system, each commodity is exchanged at its *"natural* or necessary price", which is determined by "the whole quantity of labour nature requires from man [to] produce any commodity" (1827, 219). Natural prices yield no profits and workers earn the entire value they produce. But under a regime of capitalist private property workers are paid a wage and commodities exchanged at "social prices" granting a profit. "Whatever quantity of labour may be requisite to produce any commodity, the labourer must always, in the present state of society, give a great deal more labour to acquire and possess it than is requisite to buy it from nature. Natural price thus increased to the labourer, is *social price*" (1827, 220). Profits are unjust because social prices violate natural law.

In my opinion, Marxists must reject the self-ownership axiom, chiefly because it is politically distasteful. In fact, it can be used to condemn communism as a form of exploitation of the talented by untalented people and to censure progressive redistribution policies as a form of mistreatment of the richest individuals. Not by chance, Nozick (1974) furtively uses it to justify extreme right-wing policies. Moreover, the axiom is self-contradictory. Among the various theoretical problems,[1] the following is decisive. A full property right over a thing entails the right to sell it. Therefore, a person entitled to self-ownership should have the right to sell herself as a slave. In this way, an ethical principle that seems to imply a condemnation of slavery can be used to justify it, as done by Nozick (1974, 331).

Although Marx never says that the extraction of surplus value is unjust on account of any universal principle of justice, there are some grounds for a normative interpretation of his theory of exploitation. To start with, the young-Hegelian philosopher believes that "the criticism of religion ends with the teaching that *man is the highest being for man*, hence with the *categorical imperative to overthrow all relations* in which man is a debased, enslaved, forsaken, despicable being" (Marx 1975a, 182). And even the mature economist exhibits a certain moral indignation when he declares that exploitation is "robbery", "embezzlement", "looting", "fraud" or "theft" (Geras 1985).

Moreover, although he does not like natural law philosophies, sometimes he seems to assume the self-ownership axiom. For instance, he states that a worker is the "untrammelled owner of his capacity for labour, i.e. of his person" (Marx 1996, 178). In a capitalist system, workers sell the use of their labour power. This use generates flows of abstract labour, a substance with the capacity to create value. Workers are paid a normal wage, which is lower than the quantity of abstract labour they supply in the production process. The difference is surplus value, a

---

[1] Arneson (1991) and Cohen (1995) expose all the weaknesses of the self-ownership axiom. See Philmore (alias David Ellerman) (1982) for an ironic critique. Instead of the *self-ownership* axiom, socialist reformers should adopt the rule Arrow (1973, 248) defines *asset egalitarianism*: "all the assets of society, including personal skills, are available as a common pool for whatever distribution justice calls for".

form of surplus labour; a value created by workers but appropriated by capitalists. And this looks like the moral criticism of exploitation developed by Hodgskin.

Finally, Marx gives the impression of believing that the allocation and distribution criterion prevailing in the non-exploitative system of final communism, "from each according to his ability, to each according to his needs", is an utmost principle of justice. Of course, one can take this criterion as a descriptive proposition, and contend that Marx argues that it will factually apply in communism, but not that it ought to apply (Screpanti 2013). Yet a normative reading seems to be equally defensible, if somewhat embarrassing.[2]

On the grounds of these and other clues, several philosophers have interpreted Marx's theory in normative terms.[3] Some of them resort to a Kantian notion of morality. One exemplar is Graeber (2013, 223–6), who argues that, according to Marx, capitalism is "perverse". This is because the use of labour to create value distorts "human values", produces a fetishist deformation of social relations, a commodification of labour, a mortification of the workers' creativity and, ultimately, a breach of the categorical imperative: capitalists try to use workers only as means. Another interesting example is provided by Petrucciani (2012), who proposes a moral philosophy of exploitation by reinterpreting Marx in the light of Rawls' theory of justice, which combines Kantian and utilitarian principles of morality.

Other interpretations of Marx's theory as a moral critique of the abuses of capitalism rely on the influences he was subject to during his young-Hegelian and Feuerbachian period. In this view, some principles of justice are supposed to be immanent in History, which is seen as a progression of the species-being toward self-consciousness. History has a sense because it has a potential moral subject, humankind. Capitalism is abusive as it alienates the subject, deforms his natural needs and expropriates the produce of his labour.

---

2   Embarrassing, because it is consistent with a moral justification of communism founded not on natural law, but on no less than divine law. In fact, the original postulation of the communist distribution criterion appears in the Bible (Acts 2: 44–5).

3   See Holmstrom (1977), Gould (1978), Husami (1978), Cohen (1979; 1989; 1995), Reiman (1981; 1983), Elster (1985), Peffer (1990).

Coming to modern economics, many scholars acquainted with Marx[4] have proposed refined theories of exploitation in terms of unequal exchange or undue disadvantage. These are defined as situations in which an economic agent receives something whose value is lower than what she gives in exchange or what she deserves. Injustice may spring from improper welfare or income losses, unreciprocated product flows, or the unequal distribution of asset endowments. These authors rarely trace the moral principles they adopt to judge exploitation as unjust, but they seem to assume the Aristotelian-Thomist axioms of commutative and distributive justice. Commutative justice requires that in a transaction between two individuals, neither party obtain any benefit in excess of what they give in exchange. Distributive justice prescribes the obligation to reward everyone proportionally according to their own worth. This notion is rather extensive in its possible applications. The object to be given may be power, honours, goods and so on. The "worth" yardstick might also have different facets: nobility of birth, wealth, citizenship, merit.

The problem with the two axioms is that they are not well founded as universal principles of justice. Why should workers be rewarded in accordance with their worth and why should the exchange of their labour power be an equal exchange? Because they are the owners of themselves? Or should we believe that the two axioms are implied by a natural law justification of private property in general (White 1956, 34, 40)? Marx's answer is stark: commutative and distributive justice (although he does not use these terms) are "bourgeois rights" rather than expressions of a universal moral law. He comes across the notion of "distributive justice" in the works of Pierre-Joseph Proudhon, whom he sarcastically scorns, in *The Misery of Philosophy*, as a dreamer of "eternal justice". In the same book, Marx (1976b, 142–4) scoffs at John F. Bray's ideal of equal exchange: "One hour of Peter's labour exchanges for one hour of Paul's labour: That is Mr. Bray's fundamental axiom [...]. Mr. Bray turns the *illusion* of the respectable bourgeois into an *ideal* he would like to attain [...]. Mr. Bray does not see that this egalitarian

---

4   For instance, Roemer (1982; 1994), Bowles and Gintis (1988; 1990), Roemer and Silvestre (1993), Wright (2000), Yoshihara and Veneziani (2009), Veneziani and Yoshihara (2015), Hahnel (2019). One of the first thinkers who developed such a kind of approach was the Ricardian socialist John Francis Bray (1839).

relation, this *corrective ideal* that he would like to apply to the world, is itself nothing but the reflection of the actual world."

Marx is so convinced that commutative and distributive justice are not universal moral principles, that he thinks they remain bourgeois rights even when they are implemented in the first phase of communism:

> as far as the distribution of the [means of consumption] among the individual producers is concerned, the same principle prevails as in the exchange of commodity-equivalents: a given amount of labour in one form is exchanged for an equal amount of labour in another form. Hence, *equal right* here is still in principle *bourgeois right* […]. This *equal right* is still constantly encumbered by a bourgeois limitation. The right of the producers is *proportional* to the labour they supply, the equality consists in the fact that measurement is made with an *equal standard*, labour (1989d, 86).

Then, Marx tries to account for capitalist exploitation by assuming that equal exchange prevails in a competitive market. He argues that capitalists extort surplus labour in the production process, while the circulation process is regulated by a "law of value" ensuring that "exchange is between equivalents, an equal quantity of labour for an equal quantity of labour" (Marx 1989a, 213).

If we could ask Marx to take a position on the normative theory of exploitation, I am sure he would answer that he is not interested in a moral condemnation of the abuses of capitalism (Weeks 2010). The moral philosophy he had espoused in his youth is explicitly criticised by Marx himself. In his *Marginal Notes on Wagner* (1989c), he declares that capitalist appropriation of surplus value has to be considered "just" on the grounds of the legal rules of the capitalist mode of production. By these rules, which are to be taken into account to *explain* capitalist exploitation, "surplus value rightfully belongs to the capitalist and not to the worker" (558). Marx makes it clear that his "analytic method" does not start from "man", a moral subject, but from a historically determined social system.

Hussain (2015) convincingly criticises the young-Hegelian interpretation by arguing that the materialist Marx refuses all humanist doctrines of history as a process ruled by a holistic subject. He also refuses all doctrines of the universal essence of man, the naturalness of his needs and of his productive exchange with nature. This criticism is important because it exposes the naturalism and the essentialism of some humanist and moralist readings of Marx's theory of exploitation (Screpanti 2007; 2011a).

Marx is adamant in declaring that the "just" wage in a capitalist system is that determined in the labour market. And on many occasions, he criticises the socialist doctrines based on universal principles of justice, which–in the *Critique of the Gotha Program*–he defines "dogmas", "verbal rubbish" and "ideological trash". Marx's Hegelian heritage plays a crucial role in justifying his "realist" approach. He makes the most of Hegel's notion of *Sittlichkeit* (customary ethical life) as a negation of *Moralität*. The latter is based on abstract and rational principles of justice, as in Kant. Marx's opinion is that universal moral norms do not exist, since all moral axioms are posited by philosophers or "utopian socialists" and reflect their preferences. *Sittlichkeit*, instead, is the expression of the conventional rules prevailing in certain cultures.[5] Customary ethical norms do exist, but are historically contingent. They provide practical justifications for the sentiments determining social action.

Such a vision induces Marx to adopt a descriptive approach to ethical as well as political and economic problems,[6] and in particular, a descriptive approach to the theory of exploitation. The production of profits in a capitalist system is a real, objective fact. Its understanding in term of workers' exploitation is a subjective practice, the practice whereby a social subject, an organised group of revolutionary workers, forms its own class consciousness. Such an understanding does not follow from an a-priori philosophical position. It stems from real processes involving the identification of class interests. It is not univocal, and is affected by class struggle on the ideological front. And although it is socially shaped, in the sense that individuals belonging to different classes are predisposed to accept alternative ethical beliefs, it does not spring deterministically from class structure. No social position can prevent a labourer from believing she is a free commodity seller rather

---

5 Weirdly, *Sittlichkeit*, according to Hegel, is also a dialectical synthesis of *Moralität* and *Recht*. Hegel reintroduces a normative approach to morality when he interprets History as a dialectical process ruled and finalised by Rationality.

6 Engels (1987; 1988; 1990) elaborates this approach more systematically than his friend does. Among the scholars who refuse the interpretation of Marx as a moralist critic of capitalism, see Tucker (1969), Wood (1972; 1984), McBride (1975), Miller (1984).

than a subjugated and exploited wageworker, or to think that profits are the just reward of the capitalists' contribution to production.

Summing up, there is a fundamental ambivalence in Marx's theory of exploitation, as this has both a normative and a descriptive connotation, although the latter is prevalent. It involves two approaches that are incompatible with each other, and requires the interpreter to make an unequivocal choice between them.

My personal choice endorses the descriptive approach, and sees the above-mentioned moralist propositions as simply expressing sentiments typical of a worker's point of view, as interpreted by Marx. Do not forget that besides being a social scientist, he is also the General Secretary of the International Workingmen's Association, i.e. the leader and spokesman of a revolutionary organization of workers. He is therefore entitled to construe their sentiments, claims and goals, and help bring them to fruition.

A descriptive approach to *Sittlichkeit* implies a sort of ethical relativism, and one could read Marx's scientific analysis of capitalism as being based on a method that resembles hermeneutics.[7] Science is not socially neutral: it is impregnated with interpretations, and these are expressions of class interests. As Ricardo develops his science adopting a bourgeois stance, Marx (1989e, 520) embraces a proletarian standpoint: the method of "scientific socialism" consists in "confining its scientific investigations to the knowledge of the social movement created by the people itself".

Yet, having established that Marx's theory proper is descriptive, not all problems are solved. There are scholars who think that, skipping any ethical judgment, a descriptive approach to exploitation should simply aim to *demonstrate* its existence. The proposition that surplus value is created by unpaid labour does not provide proof because it is an axiom. To be precise, it is equivalent to the axiom that posits that value is created by abstract labour. Evidence to provide proof would show that behind abstract labour there is concrete labour, which produces the use values of commodities; that only a part of commodities is consumed by the producers; and that another part is consumed by social classes that did not contribute to production, e.g. rentiers, speculators and capitalists.

---

7   See Jameson (1981), Dowling (1984), Jervolino (1996).

In this demonstration, exploitation emerges from the fact that workers supply a certain amount of necessary labour to produce the value of their subsistence goods and a certain amount of surplus labour to produce the value of the exploiters' consumer goods. Workers *enjoy the use values* of the former goods, whilst exploiters *enjoy the use values* of the latter. Notice that, in such reasoning, commodities must be *consumer* goods, for exploitation is defined in terms of welfare distribution. Investments represent a use of current output that contributes to increasing future consumption. Since we wish to avoid any ethical judgment, we raise no question about who is the legitimate owner of surplus value and who has the legitimate power to decide on investments. We only consider the effects of income distribution and investment decisions on the goods consumed by the workers and the exploiters, in both the present and the future. If all consumption accrues to the workers, there is no exploitation.

Then, imagine a system of "pure capitalism" in which the workers consume their entire wages and the capitalists invest their entire earnings. In this case, necessary labour produces the workers' current consumption and surplus labour serves to increase their future consumption. There is no exploitation, because all final products go to the workers, sooner or later.[8]

In fact, consider the case of a socialist economy in which the minister of production, as an agent of the workers, decides to earmark a part of the current output and invest it. The managers of socialist enterprises are paid a salary for their organizational activity. There is no difference from the case of a capitalist system in which the "functioning capitalists" are paid a "wage of management" (Marx 1998, chapter 23; Screpanti 1998), and in which all "profit of enterprise" exceeding this wage is invested.

In the long run, investment activity may further the escalation of real wages and grant "a constant growth of the mass of the labourers means of subsistence" (Marx 1996, 523). Actually, "a noticeable increase in wages presupposes a rapid growth of productive capital. The rapid

---

[8] See Samuelson (1971), Von Weizsäcker (1971; 1973), Vicarelli (1981).

growth of productive capital brings about an equally rapid growth of wealth, luxury, social wants, social enjoyments" (1977, 216).

This means that reinvested surplus value is not misuse from the point of view of the workers' welfare, and that exploitation boils down to the consumption capitalists enjoy in excess of their wages of management. A Saint-Simonian notion of exploitation applies in this approach: there is exploitation whenever some idle classes enjoy goods they did not contribute to producing. It is not by chance that the "working" or "industrial" class, according to Saint-Simon, includes the entrepreneurs.

Marx's view is different: all surplus value is a result of exploitation, independently of how it is spent. In a capitalist system, there is exploitation even if all profits are spent under the urge to "accumulate, accumulate!" What really matters is the identification of the social subject who controls surplus labour: "transformation of profit into capital is no more than employing a portion of excess labour to form new, additional means of production. That this takes place in the shape of a transformation of profit into capital signifies merely that it is the capitalist rather than the labourer who *has surplus labour at his disposal*" (Marx 1998, 836–7).[9]

Those who control the production process take the production decisions, regulate the exertion of labour activity and decide the expenditure of surplus value. In a socialist system, a part of the output can be saved, but its control is assigned to the workers, and there is no exploitation; in a capitalist system, control of surplus value pertains to the capitalists and there is exploitation.

In any case, Marx the scientist does not aim to *demonstrate* the existence of exploitation. He endeavours to *explain* it, and does so by bringing to light its social footing. He seeks to account for how surplus value is extracted within the legal and ethical system typical of capitalism and on the grounds of its institutions and social relations.

The gist of the explanation is as follows. Abstract labour is the labour time a worker spends in a capitalist production process. The capitalist dominates this process because the worker has entered into a contract of subordinate employment. The worker "freely" accepts this contract.

---

9 The italicised words come from David Fernbach's translation (Marx 1981). The International Publishers edition uses the words "disposes of excess labour".

She is not a slave; she is a legal entity endowed with freedom of contract. However, normal wages do not enable her to save the income she could use to earn a living autonomously. Therefore, the worker's legal freedom is spoiled by the permanent state of need that compels her to accept wage labour. In other words, the worker is not free not to accept the employment relationship (Laibman 2015, 22; Yoshihara 2017, 633). Subsequently, her real freedom to choose is cancelled out in the labour process, in which she is subject to the capitalist's power (Screpanti 2011b). This is the core of capitalist exploitation: the employer's power compels the worker to produce commodities whose value is greater than her wage, and that same power grants control of the product of labour activity.

The problem is that, probably due to the fundamental ambivalence concerning the descriptive/normative attitude, Marx expounds his theory without resolving certain ambiguities when dealing with abstract labour, exchange value and the use of labour power. This book seeks to disentangle them.

In chapter 1, I present the *pars destruens* of my interpretation. Abstract labour is a logical category defined via an intellectual process of abstraction from the characteristics of concrete labour. On the other hand, Marx also sees it as a real thing and often treats it as a natural force that creates value. This is a sort of metaphysics of value creation, expressed with a metaphor taken from the labour process: an "expenditure of human brains, nerves, muscles", which, however, are aspects of concrete labour. A series of inconsistencies ensues, that impair the labour theory of value. Besides the vices of essentialism and naturalism, the thorniest problem is caused by the fact that labour values are variables of a purely technological nature, as they only depend on the technical coefficients of production. Not by chance, Marx defines them as manifestations of a productive force operating in a system of "commodity production in general" rather than as expressions of capitalist social relations.

In chapter 2, I develop the *pars construens* of my interpretation, and argue that most of such inconsistencies can be disposed of, provided that the concept of abstract labour is interpreted in the light of what Marx writes in the *Economic Manuscript of 1861–63* and in *Results of the Direct Production Process*. In these works, he expounds the notions of "subordination" and "subsumption" and opens a new path to the theory of the employment relationship. The former notion is defined as the subjection of the worker to the capitalist, that is, the worker's obligation to execute labour activity under the command of the employer. The latter is meant as the appropriation of labour's productive power by capital, that is, the manifestation of labour capacities as attributes of capital. Here, Marx considers "irrational" the idea that a worker is a commodity seller. Instead, he characterises the employment contract as an agreement establishing a relationship of subordination. He puts forward, far in advance of the modern theory of relational contracts, the notion of the employment contract as an institution that generates an authority relationship. In this view, abstract labour is indeed a *real* abstraction, but one that emerges from a social relation, not from a natural substance: it is the labour time a wageworker spends in a production process under the command of a capitalist.

In chapter 3, I focus on exploitation and argue that it is carried out through the capitalist control of the labour process. Moreover, I show that labour values do not play any role in determining the production of surplus value and that a theory of value only serves as an instrument of measurement. On the one hand, Marx explains the production of surplus value by investigating the management of the labour process under formal and real subsumption. On the other hand, he does so by examining the vicissitudes of class struggle within and outside the factories. Class struggle plays a decisive role in determining the dynamics of labour productivity and wages — in other words, the rate of surplus value.

In chapter 4, I try to bring to light the fundamental reason why the labour theory of value is problematic. The reason is deeper than what emerges in the transformation problem. It is not so much that a uniform profit rate prevails with production prices, but rather that a profit rate exists. In fact, labour values are determined independently of profits. They hold in a non-capitalist economy and are therefore unsuitable for measuring surplus value. Fortunately, the theory of exploitation does not depend on the labour theory of value and can be expounded by resorting to production prices.

Almost all Marxists have now accepted this truth. Most of them have been convinced by a "new interpretation" which has been able to translate the value of net output into an amount of living labour and the rate of surplus value into a ratio between unpaid and paid labour. What produced such a result is the use of labour productivity as a numeraire. Another way to measure exploitation in labour units is to normalise prices with the wage, thus defining them as labour commanded. I expound these arguments in chapter 5, but not before bringing to light two paradoxes that emerge when values are determined in embodied labour. One concerns the inability of labour values to account for technical change in a capitalist economy; the other is caused by Marx's definition of equal exchange.

1. Abstract Labour as a Natural Substance

In the 1857 introduction to the *Grundrisse*, Marx argues that scientific investigation starts from the historical and empirical data the scientist assumes as "effective presuppositions". These data are a complex representation of concrete reality and are what has to be explained. Scientists, by means of abstraction, posit simple categories that identify the profound essence of the surface appearance of things. They then use these abstractions to posit and explain concrete facts, going from the essence back to its phenomenal manifestations. Explanation works as a theoretical reconstruction, based on abstract categories, of the many determinations of effective presuppositions. "But", Marx asks, "have not these categories also an independent historical or natural existence preceding that of the more concrete ones?" (1986a, 39).

His answer is: "*Ça dépend*". He thinks that some abstract notions may correspond to real facts and that in capitalism this possibility is attained in the category of "abstract labour". "Labour", he claims, "seems to be a very simple category ... Considered economically in this simplicity, 'labour' is just as modern a category as the relations which give rise to this simple abstraction" (40). He is quite explicit about the real existence of abstract labour: "In the most modern form of the bourgeois society ... the abstract category 'labour', 'labour as such', labour sans phrase, the point of departure of modern economy, is first seen to be true in practice" (41).

Now, if certain categories have "an independent historical or natural existence", then abstract labour could be considered real in a natural sense. For example, it may be described as a generic material activity implemented by labour in the transformation of nature (Kicillof and Starosta 2007a, 23; 2007b, 16). Thence, the physiological force expended in production is a natural abstraction that becomes social when commodities are exchanged (Robles-Bàez 2014, 295). Interpreted like that, the theory of abstract labour seems to give rise to a sort of a physicalist metaphysics as it postulates that the category "labour", posited by a process of logical abstraction, is incarnated in a natural substance capable of positing its own presupposition in the real world. Heinrich (2004, 2) stigmatises this as a "substantialist-naturalist theory of value".

However, if real abstraction is interpreted as the result of a historical process (Finelli 1987; 2005; Toscano 2008), it is not such an arcane thing. Abstract labour here becomes a presupposition of capitalist production, implying an overcoming of the social relationships based on personal bonds (slavery, serfdom) and the establishment of wage labour as a fundamental institution of capitalism.

In the present chapter, I seek to resolve the "ambivalence" or "ambiguity"[1] of Marx's characterization of abstract labour. I show the inconsistencies caused by attributing natural properties to it, and criticise what Postone (1978; 1993) defines as a "trans-historical" account of abstract labour. This is the *pars destruens* of my interpretation.[2]

In section 1, I reconstruct the method Marx uses to identify abstract labour in the first two parts of *Capital*, volume 1. In part 1, he defines abstract labour by distinguishing it from concrete labour and treating it as a productive force, that is, a substance that creates the value of commodities. However, he determines abstract labour within a system of "simple commodity production" that abstracts from capitalism and the wage relationship. In part 2, he introduces capital and the wage and treats abstract labour as a substance supplied by workers in a capitalist production process. This substance is appropriated by capitalists

---

1   See Heinrich (2004, 8), Bonefeld (2010, 257), Okada (2014, 409) and Robles-Bàez (2014, 292).
2   The *pars construens* is expounded in the next chapter. These two chapters re-elaborate arguments already developed in Screpanti (2017).

by the purchase of a commodity, the use value of labour power. The employment contract, in part 2, is seen as an agreement involving commodity exchange.

I deal with the notion of labour as a substance in section 2, where I argue that it can be considered a "natural" substance only when it is investigated within a model of simple commodity production or production in general. This substance is often regarded as a flow emanating from a stock of labour power embodied in the worker's organism. Thus, it is characterised as a natural force. I contend that the very attempt to treat it in this way makes it prisoner of concrete labour.

Then, in section 3, focusing on the notions of "value substance" and "value form", I observe that Marx's use of the Aristotelian notions of "substance" and "form" does not aid the understanding of abstract labour as a concept. Moreover, the idea that labour creates value sometimes induces Marx to use certain metaphors in an inaccurate way and to improperly postulate a causal relationship between the substance and the form of value.

Finally, in section 4, I argue that the treatment of abstract labour as a productive force is the main reason behind the inconsistencies which emerge in the transformation of labour values into production prices. Since labour values are determined by abstracting from capitalism, they are unable to measure correctly the capitalist exploitation of wageworkers.

1.1. The Double Abstraction

Marx (1996, 48) develops an analysis of abstract labour as a "value-creating substance" in part 1 of the first volume of *Capital* in particular, where he identifies it on the grounds of two abstraction procedures: a methodological and a substantive one.

Value is defined at the highest level of generality, that is to say, by referring it to simple commodity production, a "mode of production in which the product takes the form of a commodity, or is produced directly for exchange". This is supposed to be "the most general and most embryonic form of bourgeois production" (93). In reality, as highlighted by Lippi (1979), Marx postulates a hypothetical system of "production in general", a production process "common to all social conditions, that is, without historical character" (Marx 1986a, 245–6). In this system, capital is not yet a social relationship but "appears to be a mere thing, and entirely to coincide with the matter of which it consists" (437) or with its labour content.

Such a notion of "production in general" occurs in various works, especially the *Grundrisse* and *A Contribution to the Critique of Political Economy*. Sometimes Marx uses it to criticise theories of value that abstract from capitalism and history. However, he himself resorts to this abstraction procedure to define value and even to determine the value of capital as labour embodied in the means of production:

> The relation of capital, in accordance with its content, to labour, of objectified labour to living labour–in this relation where capital appears as passive towards labour, it is its passive being, as a particular substance, that enters into relation with labour as creative activity–can in general only be the relation of labour to its objectivity, its physical matter–which must be dealt with already in the first chapter which must precede that on exchange value and must treat of production in general (224–5).

Thus, Marx (1996, 70) builds a model of society in which "the dominant relation of man with man is that of owners of commodities". In other words, a model of society based on the production and exchange of commodities, but not on capitalist exploitation: "Commodity production in general" is production "without capitalist production" (Marx 1987, 159). In a letter to Engels, Marx (1983, 368) clarifies that, at this level of analysis, he abstracts from capital as a social relation: the "instalments [of *A Contribution to the Critique of Political Economy*] contain nothing as yet on the subject of capital, but only the two chapters: 1. The Commodity, 2. Money or Simple Circulation". Consequently, he also abstracts from the wage: "Wage is a category that, as yet, has no existence at the present stage of investigation" (Marx 1996, 54n).

In other words, Marx uses this method to isolate the determination of value from capitalist social relations. There is an explicit methodological purpose: to study value and labour at the highest level of generality. Yet the real motive is another one: to identify abstract labour as the sole productive force capable of producing value; as the sole value-creating substance. In fact, Marx believes that this level of analysis is necessary to ascertain that value is produced not by exchange but by abstract labour in the production process. In another section below, I recall the problem in Ricardo's value theory that induces Marx to use the methodology of abstraction based on "commodity production in general". Meanwhile, note that this approach defines the real abstraction of labour by reducing social activity to commodity exchange (Sohn-Rethel 1978, 20, 26; Toscano 2008, 281), and it determines value as a generic variable pertaining to the reproducibility of commodities (Ahumada 2012, 844).

Within this level of analysis, Marx delves into another procedure of abstraction; one that is substantive rather than methodological. The exchange value of commodities does not depend on the concreteness of their use values. Thus, labour as its substance cannot consist of concrete labour. Yet it cannot be a merely conceptual abstraction. Since value is an objective reality, the labour that creates it must also be a real abstraction. Abstract labour so defined is a value-creating substance in that it is a productive force. Productive labour in general (Starosta 2008, 28) is the sole productive force that produces new value:

> If the special productive labour of the workman were not spinning, he could not convert the cotton into yarn, and therefore could not transfer the values of the cotton and spindle to the yarn. Suppose the same workman were to change his occupation to that of a joiner, he would still by a day's labour add value to the material he works upon. Consequently, we see, first, that the addition of new value takes place not by virtue of his labour being spinning in particular, or joinering in particular, but because it is labour in the abstract, a portion of the total labour of society; and we see next, that the value added is of a given definite amount, not because his labour has a special utility, but because it is exerted for a definite time. On the other hand, then, it is by virtue of its general character, as being expenditure of human labour power in the abstract, that spinning adds new value (Marx 1996, 210–1).

Thus, abstract labour is defined by ignoring the specific qualities of the workers' labour activities, their skills, competencies, and performances. It is seen as a purely quantitative magnitude. Concrete labours are accordingly characterised in qualitative terms. They differ in various aspects, which can be reduced to three dimensions: (1) differences in the kinds of competencies (e. g., between those of a carpenter and those of a bricklayer), (2) differences in the complexity of competencies (e. g., between those of a bricklayer and those of an architect), and (3) differences in the degrees of performance efficiency (e. g., between the work a of carpenter who produces a table in one day and that of a carpenter who produces one in two days).

Capital and the wage are not introduced until part 2 of *Capital*, volume 1. Chapter 6 focuses on the employment contract, defining it as an agreement for "the sale and purchase of labour power":

> In order that our owner of money may be able to find labour power offered for sale as a commodity, various conditions must first be fulfilled. The exchange of commodities itself implies no other relations of dependence than those which result from its own nature. On this assumption, labour power can appear upon the market as a commodity, only if, and so far as, its possessor, the individual whose labour power it is, offers it for sale, or sells it, as a commodity. In order that he may be able to do this, he must have it at his disposal, must be the untrammelled owner of his capacity for labour, i.e. of his person (178).

Under this type of contract, the worker receives the value of labour power as payment. He is the owner of a real asset, "labour power or capacity for labour", a thing consisting of "the aggregate of those mental and physical capabilities existing in the physical form, the living personality, of a human being" (Marx 1976a, 270).[3] He sells the use value of this asset, which thus acquires a new characterization. Besides being a substance that creates the value of commodities, now it is a commodity in itself. As such, it has an exchange value and a use value. "Its use-value consists in the subsequent exercise of its force" (Marx 1996, 184). Note, incidentally, that what Marx usually labels "labour power" (Arbaitskraft) he occasionally calls "labour capacity" or "capacity for labour" (Arbeitsvermögen, Arbeitsfähigkeit). Moreover, he sometimes uses "labour" as an abbreviation for "labour capacity".

1.2. Labour as a Natural Abstraction

In another definition, the use value of labour power consists of the capacity of abstract labour to "crystallise" or "congeal" into the value of a good (50, 55, 61, 200) so that "all surplus value [...] is in substance the materialization of unpaid labour" (Marx 1994, 534). This use value

---

3   This quotation is from the Penguin edition of *Capital*, which gives a better translation than the International Publishers edition, from which I take most of the other quotations. The original phrase is: "Unter Arbeitskraft oder Arbeitsvermögen verstehen wir den Inbegriff der physischen und geistigen Fähigkeiten, die in der Leiblichkeit, der lebendigen Persönlichkeit eines Menschen existieren". From here on, when the Penguin edition provides a better translation, I quote from it.

ensues from an expenditure or use of the labour power owned by a worker. In fact

> productive activity, if we leave out of sight its special form, viz., the useful character of the labour, is nothing but the expenditure of human labour power [...]. The value of a commodity represents human labour in the abstract, the expenditure of human labour in general [...] It is the expenditure of simple labour power, i.e., of the labour power which, on average [...] exists in the organism of every ordinary individual (Marx 1996, 54).

It is evident that Marx is talking about a flow when he defines this use value as "human labour power in its fluid state, or human labour" (Marx 1976a, 142) and when he observes that it "manifests itself only in the actual usufruct, in the consumption of the labour power" (1996, 185). In fact, "the purchaser of labour power consumes it by setting the seller of it to work. By working, the latter becomes in actuality what before he only was potentially, labour power in action" (187). Marx is meticulous in arguing that "the owner of the labour power [...] must constantly look upon his labour power as his own property, his own commodity, and this he can only do by placing it at the disposal of the buyer temporarily, for a definite period of time. By this means alone can he avoid renouncing his right of ownership over it" (178). Obviously, the worker can remain the owner of labour power, notwithstanding his sale of it, only if it is a stock. What is actually sold is the usufruct of a flow.

This flow seems to be endowed with a creative power:

> Human labour creates value, but is not itself value. It becomes value only in its congealed state, when embodied in the form of some object. In order to express the value of [...] linen as a congelation of human labour, that value must be expressed as having objective existence, as being a something materially different from the linen itself, and yet a something common to the linen and all other commodities (Marx 1996, 61).

Thus, considering the various definitions introduced so far, abstract labour turns out to be: a flow emanating from a labour power that is a physical thing; a fluid that congeals into an objective form; a power that creates an objective value. Hence, the flow itself is an objective magnitude. Is it objective in a physical sense? Alas! Abstract labour is often characterised as a physical force, and the use value of labour power as the "exercise of its force" (184). For instance, it is defined as "a productive expenditure of human brains, nerves, muscles" and an expenditure of the simple labour power that "exists in the organism of every ordinary individual" (54); as "an expenditure of human labour power in a physiological sense" or "the aggregate of those mental and physical capabilities existing in the physical form, the living personality, of a human being" or the "labour power which exists only in his living body" (Marx 1976a, 137, 270, 272).

Understandably, some commentators have used these definitions to reduce the value-creating substance of abstract labour to the expenditure of bodily energy (Kicillof and Starosta 2007b, 17). They are in good company, since Marx (1986a, 393) himself declares that "what the free worker sells is always only a particular, specific measure of the application of his energy. Above every specific application of energy stands labour capacity as a totality". According to this view, abstract labour is the supply of human energy in productive activity (Kicillof and Starosta 2007a, 20). After all, "muscles burn sugar" (Haug 2005, 108; see also Starosta 2008, 31).

However, the most careful theoreticians of the value form have stigmatised such interpretations, observing that the definition of abstract labour as the expenditure of a physiological force leads to a rough understanding of value and to the loss of the social character of labour activity (Eldred and Hanlon 1981, 40).[4] In plain English, "muscles do not burn sugar in the abstract" (Bonefeld 2010, 266). According to Sraffa, the "conception that attributes to human labour a special gift of determining value" is "a purely mystical conception"; the theory of value must do "away with 'human energy' and such metaphysical things".[5]

---

[4] This assessment is expounded in different ways by Rubin (1972, 132n), Himmelweit and Mohun (1978, 80) and De Vroey (1982, 44).

[5] Unpublished papers (D3/12/9: 89 and D3/12/42: 33). See Kurz and Salvadori (2010) and Gehrke and Kurz (2018). The former of the above criticisms is raised against Marshall, the latter against Ricardo and Marx. What is stigmatised, in both cases, is a Ricardian vestige. In a letter to Tania Schucht for Gramsci, dated 21 June1932, Sraffa (1991, 74) writes that "Ricardo, contrary to the philosophers of praxis [i.e. the Marxists], never bent to historically ponder his own thought. In general, he never takes a historical point of view and, as it has been said, he considers the laws of the society in which he lives as natural and immutable laws. He was, and ever

At any rate, an energy theory of abstract labour is incongruous. In fact, the supply of energy or force–or the expenditure of brains, nerves and muscles–pertains to concrete labour, exactly the stuff from which abstraction is done. And it is easy to see that two workers who carry out different concrete labours of the same degree of complexity, and who therefore receive the same hourly wage–for instance, a call centre operator and a mechanical fitter–supply different kinds and quantities of energy and different forms and quantities of brain, nerve and muscle expenditure. Yet their abstract labours must have the same magnitude. To sum up, several definitions which Marx puts forward in part 1 of *Capital*, volume 1, lead to a characterization of abstract labour as a physical reality, a natural substance. This, however, pertains to properties of concrete labour.

1.3. Value Form and Substance

In chapter 1 of *Capital*, Marx refers to Aristotle's conception of the relationship between matter, or substance, and form.[6] Abstract labour is the substance of value and value is a form; the substance creates something that takes the form of value. He acknowledges the scientific merits of Aristotle's analysis of value and his intuition that money is a development of the simple value form. However, he also ascribes to the Greek philosopher a shortcoming: Aristotle did not understand that a common substance underlies the value equivalence among different commodities. Marx justifies him by arguing that he could not understand this truth since there was no abstract labour in the slave economy in which he lived. In fact, the common substance is none other than the abstract labour that "materialises" itself into the value form.

According to Engelskirchen (2007a; 2007b), who overtly follows an Aristotelian approach, the "structural cause" or "material cause" of the value form is the market system by which the products of labour are

---

       remained, a stockbroker of mediocre culture [...]. From his writings it is evident, so it seems to me, that their sole cultural element derives from the natural sciences".
6   Some confusion may arise because Marx often uses the term "substance" with the meaning Aristotle gives to "matter". But "matter" is only one aspect of "substance" for the Greek philosopher; another aspect is "form", and a third is the union of matter and form (see Suppes 1974; Gill 1989; Kincaid 2005).

exchanged as commodities. This interpretation, however, only accounts for the reason why commodities have an exchange value and does not clarify that value is created by abstract labour. The latter is an important proposition for Marx, but it raises two problems, as it seems to postulate: 1) an identity relationship between value and embodied labour, 2) a causal relationship between the substance and the form of value.

Regarding the first problem, see chapter 4 below. Here, I limit myself to a few remarks. According to some interpreters, Marx's analysis of the value form aims to *prove* that abstract labour is the substance of value. The reasoning seems to go as follows: if two commodities have the same exchange value, it is because they have a common substance; this can only be the abstract labour used to create their value, as would be proved by the fact that the value magnitude of the two commodities coincides with the quantity of labour contained in them. In a few words, "products can only be measured by the measure of labour–by labour time–because by their nature they are labour" (Marx 1986a, 532).

Now, the fact that 20 kilos of coffee exchange for 10 meters of fabric does not imply that the two commodities have some substance in common. It only means that coffee and fabric are exchanged at the ratio p_f/p_c=(20 kg coffee)/(10 m fabric), from which p_f(10 m fabric)=p_c(20 kg coffee), where p_f and p_c are the prices of fabric and coffee. The denomination of value in terms of money does not change this fact. In theory, money can be an arbitrarily chosen numeraire: the dollar, the price of gold, of wheat, and so on. It can be the price of labour, w=1, in which case it might happen that v_c(20 kg coffee)=(40 h labour), where v_c=2, is the labour embodied in a kilo of coffee (with zero profits) or the labour commanded by it (with positive profits). Here, the identification of the value magnitude as a quantity of embodied labour is a result of the restrictive hypothesis of zero profits. Therefore, the proposition that abstract labour is, in general, the substance of value is not proved. It has to be assumed axiomatically (Arthur 2001, 34), and Marx assumes it in the first pages of *Capital*, in which the zero-profits hypothesis is implied by the model of simple commodity production.

With regard to the second problem, can the relationship between the substance and the form of value be a proper causal relationship? The answer is no. One could say that the "material cause" of a table as a concrete object is the timber it is made of, meaning that timber is the matter (or the substance) of the table (Reuten 2005, 84). But is it sensible to argue that timber is the "efficient cause" of the table? That is, that timber is the cause of a process that produces the table as an effect?

What one can say is that the concrete labour of a carpenter produces the table in the labour process. Then, one could wrongly believe that it is possible to use a metaphor that presents abstract labour as an action that produces the value form as an effect. Actually, Marx sometimes expresses the substance-form relationship in terms of the dynamic movement of a substance from "potency" to "act" that results in the production of a form. This appears to occur as the "effect" of a "power" which is its efficient cause: "As an effect, or as inert being, of the power which produced it" (Marx 1986a, 532). Thus, it seems that labour creates value, that the value of a table is created by the abstract labour of the carpenter. Indeed, when he says that labour creates value, Marx metaphorises the labour process into the valorisation process. Yet forcing the notion of "efficient cause" in this way is not correct.

A scientifically valid metaphor must be reducible (Accame 2006). A metaphor is a linguistic construct that uses a signifier taken from another construct. It is reducible when it is possible to single out similitudes between the two constructs that can be decoded in terms of physical or mental operations. For instance, if I say, "an artist creates a picture", and then, "a carpenter creates a table", in the second proposition I am using the term "creates" metaphorically. I can reduce this metaphor to observable and comprehensible similitudes between the two propositions: "artist" is likened to "carpenter", as they have in common the condition of being people who use instruments to transform matter; "picture" is likened to "table" in that they are objects produced by human activity. Therefore, the term "creates" in the second proposition has a comprehensible meaning. This meaning adds to knowledge, for "creates" is not a simple synonym of "produces": you can say a carpenter creates a table if you mean that he not only produces a rough object of use but also puts a surplus of aesthetic worth into it.

According to Vaccarino (1988), many metaphors are irreducible as they contain a false similitude, that is, a comparison based on the negation of physical or mental operations or characteristics. So, "God created the universe" is irreducible, for "God" is defined not on the ground of characteristics possessed in common with "artist" or "man" but on the ground of characteristics that negate those of man (eternity, infinity, omniscience, omnipotence, omnipresence, etc.). These are not reducible to physical or mental operations. The proposition "God created the universe" is a metaphor devoid of any scientifically acceptable meaning.

The metaphor "abstract labour creates value" is irreducible for this same reason. One can say, "the concrete labour of a carpenter creates a table as a concrete object". However, if one says, "the abstract labour of the carpenter creates the value of the table", one is using an irreducible metaphor because abstract labour is defined as a negation of concrete labour: no characteristics of abstract labour can be likened to characteristics of concrete labour, and none is reducible to physical or mental operations. On the other hand, if to avoid a purely negative definition of abstract labour, one also attempts an operational definition in terms of energy or physical effort or the expenditure of brains, nerves and muscles, one falls into contradiction. In fact, as already observed, the expenditure of these kinds of effort pertains to concrete labour. Summing up, the meaning of "creates" in the metaphor of value creation by abstract labour is obscure and devoid of any scientific merit.[7]

1.4. Abstract Labour as a Productive Force

Marx says that "value is a relation between persons [...] concealed beneath a material shell" (1976a, 167) and that exchange value "causes the social relations of individuals to appear in the perverted form of a social relation between things" (1987, 275). Again, "the value of commodities is the very opposite of the coarse materiality of their substance, not an

---

7   This difficulty cannot be avoided by substituting the term "create" with "posit", as suggested by Arthur (2001, 40–1). Marx uses different words to convey the idea that labour produces value. On some occasions he uses *setzen* (posit); more often he uses *schaffen* (create). In *Capital*, he also uses *bilden*, which can be translated with "make", "form", "shape", "establish", "create". A problem with the term "posit", if it is not interpreted as a simple synonym of "create", is its reference to a logical procedure–like "postulate" or "hypothesize"–so that it tends to generate idealist hypostatization when referring to a real process. At any rate, would this term improve understanding? To say as Arthur does that "the abstract objectivity of value mediates itself in the abstract activity of value positing", or that "value posits itself as a quantity of negating activity fixed as what is posited", does not render Marx's metaphor more reducible, let alone, more comprehensible.

atom of matter enters into its composition [...] the value of commodities has a purely social reality" (1996, 57). These propositions convey the notion of value as a social relation. Labour value, as an essence that manifests itself in the appearance of commodity relations, should reveal to scientific investigation the social relations of production that are concealed by circulation.

However, once determined analytically, labour values are only able to reveal the structure of "socially necessary labour". That is, the simple technical arrangement of production–precisely what is to be expected if value is determined under a model of production in general. In fact, as I will detail in chapter 4, knowledge of the technical coefficients is sufficient to determine labour values, while knowledge of the rate of exploitation is not necessary. This may vary when the power relations between classes change, but if the technical coefficients do not change, labour values remain unaltered. Thus, the labour theory of value–that is, the theory that determines the value of commodities in terms of the quantity of abstract labour used to create them–is unable to shed light on the fundamental social relationship in capitalism: that of exploitation.

The difficulty also emerges in the problem of transforming labour values into production prices. I take a closer look at this problem in chapters 4 and 5. Here, I only make a few comments. A fundamental tenet of Marx's reasoning is that the aggregate substance of embodied labour cannot be altered by the transformation, which only modifies the form. After all, the market does not add anything to the quantity of surplus value arising from the production process, since this quantity is none other than crystallised labour. Marx explicitly argues that the market, by determining the profit rate uniformity, merely redistributes surplus value among industries and cannot raise it. Otherwise, prices would not be phenomenal manifestations of the value substance, but value-creating substances in their own right. Marx maintains that there is no surplus-value creation in the circulation process. However, this expectation is frustrated by the solution of the transformation problem. It is logically possible for the overall surplus value, as calculated in a price system, to be higher (or lower) than the overall surplus value as calculated in the corresponding labour value system. The rates of surplus value determined in the two systems do not generally coincide. The reason for this incongruity is profound and significant and resides in the two valuation systems' different capacities to express the social relations of production.

Labour values are forms that express the technical conditions of production and only those social facts that affect technical conditions.[8] In contrast, production prices also express social conditions of production: any variation of class relations in the production sphere causes an alteration in production prices. Labour values and production prices exhibit this different capacity to express social relations because the former are determined in a system of simple commodity production while the latter are determined in a system of capitalist production.[9]

Marx's acceptance of the labour theory of value has been stigmatised as a residue of Ricardian naturalism (Lippi 1979). As also highlighted by some theoreticians of the value form,[10] Marx is unable to fully move on from Ricardo. On the one hand, he argues that value is a social form, on the other, he sometimes reduces the value-creating substance to a physical expenditure of labour power. In such a substantialist-naturalist approach to value, Marx remains prisoner of the classical economists (Heinrich 2004, 3).

To be sure, he tries to correct the view, entertained by some classical authors, that a productive contribution is also provided by land and capital. He argues that land and capital inputs help produce "riches" or "material wealth"–that is, the physical quantities of commodities–and that their impact on the production of new value is nil. The same is true with concrete labour. He holds that only abstract labour produces value, and believes that, to reveal this, he must assert that abstract labour is a productive force. Then, in order to identify labour as the sole value-creating substance, he determines value within a system of production in general which abstracts from profits and wages. In this way, abstract labour as a "productivist motor" (Fracchia 1995, 356) is identified as an ontological and trans-historical category pertaining to a neutrally

---

8   Obviously, technical conditions may be influenced by historical and social facts: productive organization, scientific progress, market structures, etc. However, not all social facts and relations affect technical conditions.
9   Reuten and Williams (1989, 58). See also Wolff, Callari and Roberts (1984), Amariglio and Callari (1989), Biewener (1998) and Kristjanson-Gural (2009) as attempts at developing a socially contingent value approach.
10 For instance, Rubin (1972), Backhaus (1980), Eldred and Hanlon (1981), Reuten and Williams (1989), Reuten (1993) and Arthur (2001; 2004).

evolving technology (Postone 1993)[11] in a non-capitalist production system.

Now, in Marx's theory of history, the "productive forces" consist of the physical means of production, the science incorporated into them, and the individuals who use them in the labour process, in other words, the techniques in use. Thus, the workers' abilities, as characteristics of concrete labour, should be thought of as part of the productive forces. The "social relations of production", on the other hand, consist of the institutional setting used to organise production within a historically determined economic form. An institution typical of capitalism is the employment contract. Abstract labour is also typical of capitalism, as it emerges with the wage relationship, and it should therefore be ascribed to the social relations, not to the productive forces.

Why does Marx believe it necessary to abstract from wages and profits to establish that abstract labour is the sole value-creating substance? The reason is that, in Ricardo's theory, relative values are affected by profit rate uniformity in such a way that they do not coincide with the labour embodied in commodities. This result seems to impair the very Ricardian view that the value of a commodity is determined by the labour expended in its production. To tackle this problem, Marx proposes a thorough rethinking of the theory of value in terms of an abstraction (Himmelweit and Mohun 1978, 72). He defines value in a non-empiricist way, and takes it as the causal determinant of empirical phenomena (Milios, Dimoulis and Economakis 2018, 9). Then he raises the following criticism: "Though Ricardo is accused of being too abstract, one would be justified in accusing him of the opposite: lack of the power of abstraction, inability, when dealing with the value of commodities, to forget profits" (Marx 1989a, 416). In fact, in the first chapter of Ricardo's *Principles*, "not only commodities are assumed to exist–and when considering value as such, nothing further is required–but also wages, capital, profit" (393). The latter assumption is inappropriate, according to Marx. Value has first to be determined within simple commodity production. Then–maintaining that "the sum total of [the] cost prices

---

11 Postone (1978; 1993) tries to identify the abstractness of labour as an implication of the historical specificity of capitalist social relations. However, he remains faithful to the universality of the commodity form (see also Kurz 2016). Thus, Fracchia (1995, 368) is right in observing that Postone himself uses some trans-historical categories.

of all the commodities taken together will be equal to their value [and that] the total profit will be = to the total surplus value" (415)–the prices of production, or cost prices, can be determined at a lower level of abstraction.

In another respect, it is well known that Marx (1989b, 36–7) criticises Ricardo for his inability to understand that capital is a "definite social relationship", namely, "a material condition of labour, confronting the labourer as power that had acquired an independent existence". Less well known is the fact that the same criticism can be raised against Marx's way of determining value by assuming commodity production in general.

2. Abstract Labour as a Historical Reality

The present chapter presents the *pars construens* of my interpretation of the theory of abstract labour. It begins with an elucidation of the Hegelian notion of the employment contract as an agreement for the exchange of a commodity. Hegel's view, according to which this kind of contract must be likened to the Roman institution *locatio operis*, is wrong. Marx, however, develops an alternative vision that evokes the *locatio operarum*, an agreement whereby workers take on an obligation to obey their employers. These issues are dealt with in section 1 of the present chapter.

In section 2, I argue that Marx's alternative vision is based on the notions of "subordination" and "subsumption", which are used in *Capital* but are better investigated in *Results of the Direct Production Process* and in the *Economic Manuscript of 1861–63*. With the employment contract, a worker renounces his decision-making freedom in the labour process by entering into a relationship of subordination to the capitalist. This enables capital to subsume workers' capacities and use them to secure surplus value.

Then, in section 3, I define abstract labour on the grounds of the notions of subordination and subsumption. Here, abstract labour is no longer a natural object. Rather, it emerges from a historically determined social relationship. By virtue of this characteristic, it turns out to coincide with the time spent by the wageworker in the production process.

2.1. The Labour Exchange: From Hegel to Marx

The idea of labour exchange as a commodity exchange is already present in the contract theory Hegel develops in *Elements of the Philosophy of Right*. Section 80 of this work contains a classification of the different types of contracts used in modern societies, and all cases–be it sale, donation, renting, or agency–are envisaged as agreements for the alienation of a thing: to be precise, "a single external thing" (sec. 75). The internal attributes of individuals, like their labour capacities, cannot be alienated. Thus, the exchange of labour is reduced to the *contract for services*, with explicit reference to the Roman institution *locatio operis*,[1] an agreement by which the worker sells a service produced with her labour ability.

This is a mistake, for the modern *employment contract* is equated not to *locatio operis* but to *locatio operarum*. The *locatio operis* is a contract whereby, for example, I ask a mechanic to sell me a car repair service and temporarily place the car at his disposal. The *locatio operarum* has a completely different meaning: it is the agreement used by the mechanic, as an employer, to hire an employee. It is a relational contract by which a worker-lessor (*operarius-locator*) alienates, not a good consisting of a labour service, but the authority (*potestas*) the worker has over herself. She does so by temporarily placing herself at the employer's disposal. In fact, *operarum* may be interpreted both as the plural genitive of *opera* (a day's work)–so that *locatio operarum* implies the hiring of labour time in general and not of specific services–and as the irregular plural genitive of *operarius* (labourer), in which case *locatio operarum* means the hiring of workers. From the worker's point of view, these two meanings are conveyed by the expressions *locatio operarum sui*, the letting out of one's own labour time, and *locatio sui*, the letting out of oneself (Martini 1958). Both meanings are present in the modern institution of the employment contract.

Hegel does not admit the *locatio operarum* since he postulates the endowments that constitute a person are inalienable (sec. 66). And

---

1   Hegel (1991, 112) uses the odd expression *locatio operae*, which he oddly translates as *Lohnvertrag* (*wages contract*). In any case, he defines it as the "Veräußerung meines Produzierens oder Dienstleistens", that is, "alienation of my *output* or *service*", which corresponds to *locatio operis*.

when he provides examples of the "alienation of personality", he refers to cases like slavery or serfdom. He does not recognise that the employment contract is a case of partial alienation of personal freedom. Nonetheless, he does seem to have grasped the idea when he observes that I can alienate certain particular bodily and spiritual attitudes to someone else, and that "I can give him the use of my abilities for a restricted period" (sec. 67). This is on the right track because, in the kind of rule of law prevailing in modern capitalism, the principle of the inalienability of personal freedom implies the prohibition of slavery but does not rule out the possibility that a worker signs a contract of *subordinate* employment. However, Hegel insists on the idea that what is actually alienated in such a case is only an array of single products, not a part of one's personal freedom. He maintains that wageworkers would not lose their freedom in the production process since the use of their force is different from the force itself. But then, why is it necessary to clarify that the sale of personal abilities is admitted only for a limited time? Such a qualification is necessary if the contract is intended as an agreement by which workers are surrendering their *potestas* and not yielding only single services. With the sale of *potestas* not limited in time, it would be an enslaving contract.

Hegel's argument is reproduced almost literally by Marx (1985b, 128) in *Value, Price and Profit*, where he says that a "maximum time is fixed for which a man is allowed to sell his labouring power. If allowed to do so for any indefinite period whatever, slavery would be immediately restored". Also, in *Capital*, Marx (1996, 178) says that "the continuance of this relation demands that the owner of labour power should sell it only for a definite period, for if he were to sell it rump and stump, once and for all, he would be selling himself, converting himself from a free man into a slave". More explicitly than Hegel, Marx sometimes argues that a worker is the owner of labour power and sells a certain quantity of it as a commodity. However, Marx's qualification of the temporariness of the sale is only plausible when the employment contract is understood as establishing a relationship of subordination.

Marx is certainly not afraid of bringing to light the slave-like nature of wage labour, nor is he afraid of recognizing that the worker with the employment contract "sells at auction eight, ten, twelve, fifteen hours of his life, day after day" (1977, 203). And he insists on the idea that wageworkers sell themselves. For instance, in a letter to Abraham Lincoln he says that, compared to the black slave, who is "mastered and sold without his concurrence", the white worker boasts the higher prerogative "to sell himself and choose his own master" (1985a, 20). This idea grasps the meaning of the employment contract better than the theory that reduces it to commodity sale.

The comparison Marx suggests between slavery and wage labour reveals the distance he takes from Hegel on a decisive issue. This paves the way for the development of a theory of the employment contract as an institution that generates the authority relationship required to implement capitalist exploitation.

2.2. The Subsumption and Subordination of Labour

To comprehend abstract labour as resulting from a social relation of production, it is necessary to understand the way capital appropriates living labour. In an illuminating passage of the *Grundrisse*, Marx (1986a, 205) says that, in the exchange between capital and labour,

> the use-value of what is exchanged for money appears as a *particular economic relationship*, and the specific *utilization* of what is exchanged for money constitutes the ultimate purpose of both processes [that in which the workers get the money and that in which the capitalist appropriates labour]. Thus there is already a distinction of form between the exchange of capital and labour and simple exchange [...]. The difference of the second act from the first–the *particular process of appropriation of labour* on the part of capital is the second act–is EXACTLY the distinction between the exchange of capital and labour and the *exchange of commodities* as mediated by money. In the exchange between capital and labour, the first act is an exchange and falls wholly within ordinary circulation; the second is *a process qualitatively different from exchange* and it is only BY MISUSE that it could have been called exchange of any kind at all. *It stands directly opposed to exchange.*

The words I have italicised convey three original ideas: 1) in exchange for the wage paid to the worker, the capitalist obtains the establishment of a relationship, not a thing; 2) such a relationship serves to prompt the process of the utilization and appropriation of labour; 3) this process is qualitatively different from the exchange of commodities and is its

2. Abstract Labour as a Historical Reality

direct opposite. The employment contract determines an "exchange" that is a "non-exchange" for the capitalist:

> The exchange between capital and labour, the result of which is the price of labour, even though for the worker is a simple exchange, must for the capitalist be non-exchange. He must receive more value than he has given. From the point of view of capital, the exchange must be merely apparent, i.e. an economic category other than exchange, or else capital as capital and labour as labour in antithesis to it would be impossible (247).

In what sense is this transaction, which appears to the worker as an exchange, a "non-exchange" for the capitalist, or a "merely apparent" exchange? Marx (1994, 444) answers this question in *Results of the Direct Production Process*, where he says that the worker as "the owner of labour capacity figures as its seller–irrationally expressed, as we have seen". Why irrational? Because that is how the worker appears, although not how he really is. Instead, the worker is a "direct seller of living labour, not of a commodity". Then Marx explains that "with the development of capitalist production all services are converted into wage labour, and those who perform these services are converted into wage labourers", even unproductive workers. This fact "gives the apologists [of capitalism] an opportunity to convert the productive worker, because he is a wage labourer, into a worker who merely exchanges his services" (446). In reality, no commodity consisting of a worker's service is exchanged in the "labour market". Rather, a social relationship is shaped that transforms the producer into a wageworker. Then the apologists of capitalism present the worker as a seller of services, and in this way, they make the "non-exchange" of labour appear as an exchange of commodities.

To my knowledge, Marx is not acquainted with the notion of a "contract for services". Yet he is very clear in rejecting the labour ideology, still entertained by many economists today, that represents a wageworker as the seller of labour services or, all the same, as the seller of a commodity resulting from labour activity:

> What the capitalist buys is the temporary right to dispose of labour capacity [...]. Labour *belongs* to the capitalist after the transaction, which has been completed before the actual process of production begins. The *commodity* which emerges as product from this process belongs entirely

to him. He has produced it with means of production belonging to him and with labour he has bought and which therefore belongs to him [...]. The capitalist's surplus arises precisely from the fact that he buys from the labourer not a commodity but his labour capacity itself (Marx 1989a, 212–3).

In *Results of the Direct Production Process* and the *Economic Manuscript of 1861–63*, Marx clarifies the notions of "subordination" and "subsumption".[2] These also appear in the final version of *Capital*, but not with the disruptively innovative strength they have in the *Results*. Sometimes Marx uses the two words as synonyms, sometimes as distinct terms. In any case, it is important to keep them separate and to understand the differences in their meanings. The term "subordination" denotes a relation between the capitalist[3] and the worker as employer and employee, a "relation of domination" (Marx 1994, 431) in the production process. The term "subsumption" refers to the arrangement whereby the productive power of labour becomes "a productive power of capital" (429). The firm is the legal embodiment of capital, and the productive forces deployed in the production process pertain to it, even though labour activities are executed by the workers. The firm's ownership of a worker's productive capacity originates from the

---

2   The *Economic Manuscript of 1861–63* is the second draft of *Capital*. The chapter *Results of the Direct Production Process* was intended to appear with the third draft, written in 1863–4. The version of *Capital* finally published comes from a revision of the third draft, from which, however, the chapter on the *Results* was deleted. Several scholars have raised the question of why Marx made this choice. See Murray (2016, chap. 11) for a critical survey. Skillman (2013) puts forward an appealing answer: Marx must have realised there was some inconsistency between the "value-theoretic account" of surplus value production, as expounded in the final version of *Capital*, and the "historical account", as developed in the *Economic Manuscript of 1861–63* and the *Results*. My opinion is that there is indeed an inconsistency between the explanation of exploitation based on a labour theory of value holding under "commodity production in general" and the explanation based on a historically determined social relationship, namely, the capitalist forms of subsumption and subordination–and this might be the reason why the *Results* remained unpublished. Moreover, Marx must have sensed that it is difficult to reconcile the theory of the employment contract as an agreement establishing an authority relationship with the theory (expounded in part 2 of *Capital*, volume 1) presenting it as a transaction for the sale and purchase of a commodity.

3   Subordination also occurs in pre-capitalist systems. With the passage to a capitalist mode of production a change of form takes place, as I clarify below.

"subordination to capital of the labour process" (439).[4] This ownership gives foundation to the employer's undifferentiated property of the product of work activity.

Marx (1988b 93) defines *formal* subsumption and subordination as follows: "This formal subsumption of the labour process, the assumption of control over it by capital, consists in the worker's subjection as worker to the supervision and therefore the command of capital or the capitalist. Capital becomes command over labour [...] in the sense that the worker as a worker comes under the command of the capitalist". The subsumption is formal, insofar as the individual worker, instead of working as an independent commodity owner, now works as a labour capacity belonging to the capitalist and therefore under his command and supervision (262).[5]

Here the adjective "formal" evokes the way in which, in Hegel's philosophy, a kind of contract determines a relationship only formally. That is to say, abstracted from its substantial content, from the specific characteristics of the object of exchange, and from the personal identities of the parties (Benhabib 1984). In this sense, a type of contract is an institutional condition that determines the form of a social relationship. Subsumption and subordination are formal in that they are based on

---

4   As far as I know, Marx is the first modern economist to think of the employment contract as an institution establishing an authority relationship. He does so with the theory of the *subordination* of wageworkers. See Coase (1937) and Simon (1951) for two important neo-institutional elaborations of this theory. For a refined juridical treatment, see Kahn-Freund (1972). Ellerman (1992) expounds a view based on a natural rights theory of property. Screpanti (2001) develops a Marxist formulation. Marx is also considered a precursor of the competence-based theory of the firm (Hodgson 1998). Indeed, the theory of *subsumption* of labour capacities is crucial in accounting for the prerogative of a capitalist company to appropriate and mould the workers' abilities and transform them into the firm's competences. In fact, with subsumption, "the social productive powers of labour all present themselves as productive forces, as properties inherent in capital [...]. The social combination of the individual labour capacities [...] does not belong to the workers, but rather confronts them as a capitalist arrangement" (Marx 1994, 455–6). The capitalist contributes to building organizational competences while governing individual competences in the labour process, just as a conductor determines the performance of an orchestra.

5   Murray (2004, 257) notes that Marx tends to use the expression "formal subsumption" with two different meanings: a general notion defining the constitution of the wage relationship as a legal presupposition of real subsumption; and a specific notion of *merely* formal subsumption, conceived as a historical phase preceding that of real subsumption. Clearly, the first meaning is the most important from a theoretical point of view.

the form of contract by which wage labour originates in a capitalist economy: "There is already a distinction of form between the exchange of capital and labour and simple exchange". The employment contract is the institution that enables two parties endowed with legal personality to establish voluntarily a relationship of subordinate employment: "If the relation of domination and subordination replaces those of slavery, serfdom, vassalage [...] there takes place only a change in their form" (Marx 1994, 432–3). The employment contract, i.e. "wage labour and its employment by capital", is the "dominant relation" in a capitalist mode of production (Marx 1988b, 112).

Once capital has taken control of labour, it governs labour activity in view of its goals, so that subsumption becomes real, involving the capitalist's regulation of the labour process. In fact, "The formal subsumption of labour under capital [...] is the condition and presupposition of its real subsumption". In other words, formal subsumption "is the general form of any capitalist production process" since it establishes the social relation by virtue of which "the labour process is subsumed under capital (it is capital's own process) and the capitalist enters the process as its conductor, its director" (430, 424). What the capitalist gets in exchange for the wage is the prerogative to start the second "act" or "process" of the exchange, which takes place in the factory. The employment contract creates the legal conditions for the utilization of living labour in the production process, as the contract sanctions "the appropriation of the ability to dispose over the labour" or "the appropriation of the title to its use" (Marx 1987, 506). Such title is acquired by the capitalist by virtue of the obligation to obedience taken on by the worker through the contract, and this ensures that "there develops within the production process itself [...] an economic relation of domination and subordination" (Marx 1994, 430).

The function of command in the labour process is necessary to realizing the exploitation of workers. This is so even in pre-capitalist economic forms, but there is a specifically capitalist mode of establishing the subordination of labour. In pre-capitalist economic forms, command over labour is based on relationships of "personal" bond, enforced by institutions of an eminently political and policing nature. In the capitalist mode of production, any kind of personal bond is overcome, and workers are recognised as citizens endowed with the freedom of contract. What is it, then, that ensures workers' subordination to capitalists?

The basic features of formal subsumption are these:

> (1) The purely money relation between the person who is appropriating the surplus value and the person who provides it; to the extent that subordination arises, it arises from the particular content of the sale, not from a subordination pre-posited to the sale, which might have placed the producer in a relation other than the money relation (the relation of one commodity owner to another) towards the exploiter of his labour, as a consequence of political conditions etc. It is only as owner of the conditions of labour that the buyer brings the seller into a condition of economic dependency; it is not any kind of political and socially fixed relation of domination and subordination. (2) Something implied by the first relation–for otherwise the worker would not have to sell his labour capacity–namely the fact that the objective conditions of his labour (the means of production) and the subjective conditions of his labour (the means of subsistence) confront him as capital (Marx 1994, 430).

In the market, a worker is legally free. The ideology of capital induces in him "the consciousness (or rather the idea) of free self-determination, of freedom", and this renders him a "much better worker" (Marx 1994, 435).[6] In the *Economic Manuscript of 1861–63* and in *Results of the Direct Production Process*, Marx tries to deconstruct such an ideology. He argues that, by virtue of that idea, a worker believes himself to be free, and hence justifies to himself the acceptance of the employment contract. But in reality, he is not free; rather, "he has a choice [...] as to whom he sells himself to, and can change MASTERS" (437). In other words, workers are "free" to submit to the power of their exploiters. The paradox of the employment contract is that it sanctions the formally free choice of workers to surrender their real freedom for a certain number of hours. The material condition of this paradox resides in the fact that the workers are "free" of any wealth, that is, they do not own the means of production and subsistence that would enable them to choose autonomously how to earn a living.

Once the contract is signed, workers enter the factory, where their freedom of choice is *in principle* nil and labour activity is "imposed" on

---

6   The word "idea" appears in the Penguin edition (Marx 1976, 1031); in the International Publishers edition, the word is "notion".

them (De Angelis 1996, 18–9). The workers cannot decide how to work, what to produce, how to cooperate with other workers, how to use the machines, and so on. These prerogatives pertain to the capitalist, who has used the employment contract to transform the freedom surrendered by the workers into his own power. *In practice*, the employer's authority can be limited to some extent by laws, customs, the contract itself, and especially the workers' resistance. In fact, not only the wage negotiation but also the labour process is a field of class conflict, as I will clarify in the next chapter. The struggle in the labour process is about the use of labour capacities.[7] This use pertains to the capitalist, who utilises labour power by giving instructions to the workers. The implementation of the instructions pertains to the workers, who can use collective action and information asymmetries to reduce their fatigue and exploitation (Screpanti 2011b).

Summing up, the basic scientific innovation resides in the idea that formal subsumption and subordination are necessary conditions for the extraction of surplus value in a capitalist production process. Subsumption means that the exploiter has a title to use labour capacities. Such a title is acquired by virtue of subordination, i.e. the obligation of the exploited worker to obey the exploiter's commands. This is the case in all social systems based on exploitation. In slavery, for instance, the workers' subordination is what enables a master to compel slaves to overwork. Masters have the power to use the labour capacities of their slaves to produce a surplus product because slaves are obliged to obey. What characterises a capitalist system is that subordination and subsumption are ensured by the wage relationship, as established via an employment contract.

2.3. Abstract Labour as Resulting From a Social Relationship

The absence of the expression "abstract labour" in *Results of the Direct Production Process* merits particular reflection. Despite the expression's omission, Marx deals with this concept extensively in that work. For

---

[7] De Angelis (1995; 1996) perceptively accounts for class struggle in the production process by referring it to the character of abstraction taken by wage labour as subordinate activity.

instance, when he reconstructs the historical transformation process of the artisan labour relationship into a capitalist relationship, he observes that the capital of a master artisan "is tied to a particular form of use-value". The capitalist firm, in contrast, involves "the removal of all these barriers [...]. Capital (money) can be exchanged for any kind of labour" (Marx 1994, 434–5). Subsequently, he says that "in North America, where the development of wage labour has least of all been affected by the old guild system, etc., this variability, this complete indifference to the specific content of labour [...] is shown particularly strongly" (438). He explains that in a capitalist economy labour is only productive if it produces surplus value, arguing that it "has absolutely nothing to do with the particular content of the labour, its particular usefulness or the specific use-value in which it is expressed" (448).

When talking about "abstract labour" in *Results of the Direct Production Process*, Marx never uses this expression. Rather, he speaks of "undifferentiated, socially necessary, general labour, entirely indifferent towards any particular content" (401), hence outlining the phenomenon by specifying its economic and social properties rather than its physical ones. These expressions refer to two characteristics of labour that need to be clearly distinguished: on the one hand, it is socially necessary; and on the other, it is indifferent or general.

The notion of "socially necessary labour" refers to a situation of productive efficiency. Labour with "socially normal" intensity (396) is employed in the factories in the quantities and qualities required by the technique in use. This notion shares with that of "abstract labour"–as a natural abstraction–the characteristic of being a productive force but not that of being abstract. In fact, the material base of socially necessary labour consists of concrete labours, specified in relation to production techniques. For instance, so many hours of bricklayers' labour to build houses, so many hours of engineers' labour to build cars.

The notion of "indifferent or general labour", in contrast, must be interpreted as meaning "indifference towards any particular content". It is abstracted from concrete labours and shares with abstract labour the characteristic of being quantifiable. Marx clarifies that the fundamental reason why labour becomes a quantifiable magnitude is that the worker's activity is carried out under a relation of subordination. Consequently, his productive forces, being subsumed under capital, are no longer attributes of labour. The labour characteristic of being quantifiable is intimately linked to its historicity: capitalist subsumption occurs only in a production system based on wage labour. In this way, the properties of naturalness and historicity are separated. The former pertains to the technological structure of socially necessary labour, the latter to the social structure that ensures exploitation.

In the *Grundrisse* quote I reported at the beginning of the preceding section, Marx accounts for the historical appearance of the wage relationship by arguing that capital is interested in exchanging with labour, and that the ultimate purpose of this exchange is to obtain the title to the appropriation and utilization of labour. He later makes clear that "the social productive powers of labour all present themselves as productive forces, as properties inherent in capital [...]. The social combination of the individual labour capacities [...] does not belong to the workers, but rather confronts them as a capitalist arrangement, it is inflicted upon them" (Marx 1994, 455–6).

The subsumption of labour capacities under capital is the real fact that engenders the firm's indifference toward concrete labours *from the standpoint of accountancy*. In the determination of a commodity value, wage costs are calculated in terms of the quantity of money paid per labour hour, disregarding the workers' productive forces. This is the crucial point, and Marx is fully aware of it: the wage is determined independently of labour productivity. Capitalists are very involved in the use of labour skills, as far as the management and organization of the labour process are concerned. However, in recording labour costs, they are unconcerned about the specific use values of labour, not because they are not interested in the workers' concrete abilities, but because the productive capacities associated with these abilities belong to capitalists once the employment contract is signed. What is bought, what is paid for, is not the set of these abilities and not even a generic labour capacity. It is another thing, and a truly abstract one indeed: labour time, meaning the time during which a worker undergoes the capitalist's control in the production process.

The close relationship between workers' subordination to capital and the independence of the wage from workers' specific skills and competencies can also be seen from another angle. With real subordination, capitalists exert command in the labour process, and thence the power to determine all its aspects: the method and organization of labour, the choice of techniques, the investment decisions, the use of science, and so on. This implies that capitalists also have the power to reallocate workers among various tasks in relation to technical change and even the power to reskill workers at their will. They demand from their employees a certain degree of malleability, meaning not only a willingness to obey orders but also pliability toward their exigency to reshape abilities. This is made possible by the workers' indifference to the use of their concrete labour. In fact, the workers' competences have become the firm's competences, so that it is "in the nature of the wage labour subordinated by capital that it is indifferent to the specific character of its labour and must submit to being transformed in accordance with the requirement of capital" (1998, 194).

Now it should be easier to understand why the wage is commensurate to a purely quantitative magnitude and why it is reasonable to use the concept of abstract labour to denote this magnitude, but only after purging it of any characteristic of naturalness and productiveness. Precisely this abstraction makes exploitation possible. Once the price of labour time is fixed, and once capital has subsumed the workers' capacities, it is a capitalist prerogative to manage the production process in such a way as to obtain commodities whose value added is greater than the wage paid. Capitalists' power enables them to extract a higher or lower surplus value from production; their organizational and managerial abilities determine labour productivity and therefore the intensity of exploitation. In fact, the capitalist compels the worker "to ensure that his labour possesses at least the socially normal average degree of intensity [and] will try to raise it as much as possible above this minimum and extract from him over a given period as much labour as possible, for every [increase in the] intensity of labour over the average degree creates [a bigger] surplus value for him" (Marx 1994, 396).

Remember that a *contract for services* involves the exchange of a labour *service*, a commodity, whose productivity is supposed to be known ex-ante, i.e. before the transaction is concluded. On the ground of this productivity, the market determines the service price as that which equalises demand and supply. On the contrary, labour productivity is not known ex-ante in an *employment contract,* and the "market" determines only the price of labour *time,* without any connection with labour productivity. This is determined ex-post, in the factory, and is a function of the exercise of the capitalist's power within the labour process. It is this power that enables the capitalist to extract a surplus value from labour activity.

The contract itself and the parties' bargaining powers set the price of labour time. By establishing the worker's obligation to obedience for a prearranged length of time, the contract fixes a wage that is commensurate to that time. So, to be precise, the wage is the price of freedom, a payment for obedience, and not the value of a commodity. "The more [the workers] wish to earn, the more must they sacrifice their time and carry out slave-labour, completely losing all their freedom" (Marx 1975b, 237). In the exchange with capital, workers alienate their own freedom. "What [they] receive as the price is the value of this alienation" (Marx 1986a, 248).

At last, we can understand why abstract labour is "practically true" in a social and historical sense, but cannot be so in a natural sense. This is because a historically determined social relationship enables the capitalist to treat labour *as if* it were a homogeneous input and to measure its quantity in time units. Since it is typical of the capitalist mode of production, abstract labour emerges in all its simplicity only in the most modern economic form of human evolution:

> The simple abstraction which plays the key role in modern economy, and which expresses an ancient relation existing in all forms of society, appears to be true in practice in this abstract form only as a category of the most modern society [...]. The example of labour strikingly demonstrates that even the most abstract categories [...] are, in the determinateness of their abstraction, just as much a product of historical conditions and retain their full validity only for and within these conditions. Bourgeois society is the most developed and many-faceted historical organization of production. The categories which express its relations [provide] an understanding of its structure (Marx 1986a, 42).

3. Labour Subsumption and Exploitation

A scientific theory of capitalist exploitation aims to causally explain the production of surplus value. Marx develops this theory in volume 1 of *Capital*, especially parts 3–5, which are devoted to elucidating the effects of capitalist control of the labour process, and parts 6–7, devoted to explaining the dynamics of wage determination. In fact, most of the volume deals with the social, technological and organizational conditions of exploitation.

The theory of labour subordination and subsumption is not yet an explanation of exploitation. It is a theory of the capitalists' power. It becomes the essential part of a proper explanation of exploitation through reconstruction: firstly, of the way in which that power is used in managing a factory[1] and, secondly, of the way wages are fixed.

Marx's reasoning in parts 3–5 reveals that concrete commodities are the products that workers actually *create* in the *labour process*. A

---

1   Yoshihara (1998), Veneziani (2013) and Vrousalis (2013) clarify that a theory of power is necessary to account for exploitation. Following publication of the seminal and controversial book by Braverman (1974), an important line of research known as "labour process theory" has developed in contemporary sociology, with the goal of investigating the capitalist organization of labour activity. See, for instance, Knights and Willmott (1990), Shalla and Clement (2007), and Thompson and Smith (2010). In my reconstruction, it is not necessary to enter the infinite debate provoked by Braverman's thesis on the tendency of capitalism to deskill labour activity. Suffice it to recall that an alternative view has been put forward, which holds that a skill-upgrading tendency exists. See Adler (1990) as one of the most persuasive proponents of this thesis.

commodity is a thing, an object produced by a subject using concrete labour. Value, contrarily, is not a thing, and cannot be supposed to be created by a subject. It is an economic relationship among commodities, and a result of the social relations prevailing in productive activity. This analysis can be interpreted as an instantiation of the idea that the labour process pertains to the productive forces (e.g. labour skills and technical knowledge), while the valorisation process pertains to the social relations of production (e.g. property rights, contract institutions and power systems). A capitalist's power (a social relation) is used in the factories to compel workers to produce commodities (a productive force). Exploitation occurs when the value added of commodities is higher than wages.

This seems a reasonable interpretation of the analysis developed in parts 3–5 of *Capital*, volume 1. Marx justifies it in the *Results of the Direct Production Process* when he declares that, by virtue of the workers' subordination, the *labour process* is subsumed under capital. This means that it becomes an *instrument* of the valorisation process, the place where surplus-value is "manufactured". Actually, it is in the labour process that the capitalist intervenes as a director; and it is in the labour process that he carries out the "direct exploitation" of labour:

> The labour process becomes an instrument of the valorisation process, of the process of capital's self-valorisation, the process of the manufacture[2] of surplus value. The labour process is subsumed under capital (it is capital's *own* process) and the capitalist enters the process as its conductor, its director; for him it is at the same time directly a process of exploitation of alien labour (Marx 1994, 424).

True, in parts 3–5 Marx persists in uttering that value is created as a "materialization" of abstract labour or a "transposition" of labour power. Yet, such notions do not play any role in accounting for the production of surplus value. In the analysis developed in these parts, surplus value is explained as the result of the capitalist's ability to compel workers to attain a labour productivity higher than the wage. In point of fact, the labour unit only serves as an instrument of measurement. Thus, one of the implications of the analysis reconstructed in the present chapter is

---

2   The word "manufacture", to translate *Fabrikation*, appears in the Penguin edition. The International Publishers' edition uses "creation".

that the labour theory of value is not necessary to explain exploitation. To say it with Gordon (2017, 2), "Marx's thesis of labour exploitation does not follow from the labour theory of value". In this reconstruction, exploitation is explained with an analysis of the way capitalists control the labour process and the way in which the bargaining powers of conflicting classes determine wages, labour intensity and the working day.

In section 1 of the present chapter, I expound Marx's investigation of the production of "absolute surplus value" under conditions of merely formal subsumption. The capitalist uses his power to lengthen the working day or intensify labour activity. The production of absolute surplus value is carried out without technical change and, indeed, without any need to modify the technical structure of production. The only way in which command is used in the labour process is to ensure that the workers do their jobs efficiently.

Then, in section 2, I consider the production of "relative surplus value", which is extracted by making subsumption real, i.e. by restructuring the labour process via the introduction of new techniques, the activation of increasing returns to scale, the organization of cooperation and team production, and the development of automation in large-scale industry. To simplify analysis, Marx initially assumes that socially necessary labour is determined just by the technology. Surplus value is defined as "relative" in that it is compared to a given working day. It may rise because the amount of necessary labour shrinks in relation to the number of hours worked, due to improvements in labour productivity. However, after the notion of "relative surplus value" has been elucidated, Marx removes that simplifying hypothesis. He then makes clear that the exercise of the capitalist's power within a factory is always a contested terrain, since the workers continually practice some forms of defiance and shirking behaviour, and the capitalists are compelled to enact structures of hierarchical control to quell the workers' resistance. This means that socially necessary labour, labour intensity, labour productivity and the actual working day, and therefore the degree of exploitation, are not simply determined outside the production process, i.e. by law, customs, collective agreements, and the available technology. Class struggle within the factory plays a decisive role in determining the degree of exploitation.

Finally, in section 3, I illustrate Marx's theory of wages, which is one of the most topical of his doctrines. It deals with how class struggle in the so-called "labour market" contributes to wage determination. The "labour market" is not a market proper. It is a battlefield of class struggle (by the way, this is the reason why I use inverted commas when dealing with the "labour market"). In abstract theory, Marx follows the classical economists in maintaining the "value of labour power" is fixed at a subsistence level in a competitive market. However, in most of *Capital* and in other works, he tries to explain how wages are actually affected by the dynamics of capital accumulation, the industrial reserve army and trade union activities–in short, by the bargaining powers of opposing classes. He investigates the determination of both the "market wages" in various phases of the business cycle, and the long-run trend of normal wages. The most effective weapon of the capitalists in this struggle consists of their investment decisions and the ensuing changes in the industrial reserve army, whilst the main workers' weapon consists of the industrial action they can engage in.

3.1. The Production of Absolute Surplus Value

Marx (1996, 187) begins his analysis of exploitation mechanisms by using a simple model which, like the concept of "production in general", is abstract in nature: "The fact that the production of use values, or goods, is carried out under the control of a capitalist and on its behalf, does not alter the general character of that production". This is a very abstract model indeed, as it is difficult to envisage a capitalist system in which capitalists do not really determine the technical structure of production. Yet such an abstraction might be of use to isolate some aspects of the control of labour.

Marx reasons as if there had been a historical transformation from an economy of simple commodity production to an economy in which capitalists establish formal subsumption by employing some previously independent worker. In this economy, capitalists have become owners of the means of production but have not yet modified the labour process. Imagine a situation in which a number of self-employed artisans become wageworkers but continue to produce using the techniques they used in their workshops and with no improvement in the division of labour. Now their employers have become the owners not only of the commodities they produce, but also of the use of their labour power, in other words, of the workers' competencies, because they have acquired "a title and a right to the labour and the surplus labour" (315).

Since the labour process has not changed and no new technique has been introduced, the capitalists' control is exerted only to take "good care that the work is done in a proper manner, and that the means of production are used with intelligence" (195), in other words, "that the labourer does his work regularly and with the proper degree of intensity" (314). Subsumption is merely formal, not yet real, because "capital subordinates labour on the basis of the technical conditions in which it historically finds it" (314).

In any case, an important principle is established: that, in modern industrial capitalism, formal subsumption is a necessary condition for exploitation in the production process. The capitalist pays the workers their normal wage, but then he manages them in the production process to make them produce a higher value (Murray 2004, 246).

Theoretically, the difference between an artisan workshop and a capitalist factory implies a fundamental social and economic transformation. Simple *value creation* takes place in "commodity production in general", whilst capital *valorisation*, i.e. the production of surplus value, arises in the capitalist mode of production. The question is: where does surplus value come from, if labour productivity has not changed? The answer is threefold. A capitalist can succeed in extracting surplus value by: lengthening the working day, intensifying labour activity, or lowering the wage.

Assume an artisan produces a subsistence income by working 6 hours a day, from hour a to hour b, let's say, from 6 o'clock to 12 o'clock. This is his "necessary labour", the quantity of labour necessary to reproduce his labour power. A capitalist may be willing to employ a worker in his factory if she is ready to work for more than $b-a=6$ hours. Marx provides three examples of working day, in which its length is $c-a=7$, or $d-a=9$, or $e-a=12$ hours.

Working day I: a------b-c

Working day II: a------b---d

Working day III: a------b------e

If wageworkers are paid for their necessary labour, b-a, they provide the amounts of surplus labour c-b or d-b or e-b. The quantities of commodities produced increase and all surplus labour becomes surplus value.

One could also raise the question of why a wageworker should accept to work more hours than a self-employed worker could for the same daily income. Marx's answer is that in a capitalist system there is always a certain number of unemployed people who have no capital to invest in an independent business and are therefore compelled to accept a contract of subordinate employment in order to earn a living. And a capitalist would not employ a worker who is not prepared to work for producing a profit.

Another interesting question is about how the length of the working day is established. Marx spends many pages arguing that there is no natural limit to that length, apart from 24 hours, and that "the inherent tendency" of the "vampire" capitalist is "to appropriate labour during all 24 hours of the day" (263). Fortunately, this does not happen because the workers' tendency is to work as little as possible. Therefore, the working day is determined by class struggle: "In the history of capitalist production the determination of what is a working day presents itself as the result of a struggle, a struggle between collective capital, i.e., the class of capitalists, and collective labour, i.e., the working class" (243).

Moreover, the State intervenes in social conflict by regulating the length and the arrangement of the normal working day. In doing so, it contributes to preserving the workers' wellbeing and their economic efficiency in the interests of the bourgeoisie as a class, against those of the individual vampire capitalists. In any case, it is forced to do so by the final balance of bargaining powers:

> These minutiae, which, with military uniformity, regulate by stroke of the clock the times, limits, pauses of the work, were not at all the products of Parliamentary fancy. They developed gradually out of circumstances as natural laws[3] of the modern mode of production. Their formulation, official recognition, and proclamation by the State, were the result of a long struggle of classes (1996, 287–8).

---

3   Marx often uses the expressions "natural laws" and "laws of nature", mostly with the meaning of objective laws of functioning of a historically determined social system–for instance, "the natural laws of capitalist production", or "the natural laws of a particular form of production".

Another method for increasing the production of absolute surplus value is to intensify labour activity. The most effective modes of labour intensification occur in the production of relative surplus value, i.e. through changes in techniques and organization. But there is a way that seems manageable even under merely formal subsumption. That is, if the length of the working *day* cannot be increased, the length of the actually worked *hour* can, e.g., by cutting the customary or legally sanctioned pauses for eating, rest etc. This practice is equivalent to a lengthening of the working day.

In the *Results of the Direct Production Process* Marx observes that the capitalist compels the worker

> to ensure that his labour possesses at least the socially normal average degree of intensity [and] will try to raise it as much as possible above this minimum and extract from him over a given period as much labour as possible, for every [increase in the] intensity of labour over the average degree creates [a bigger] surplus value for him (Marx 1994, 396).

In other words, capitalists can force the workers to work *harder*. It is dubious whether this practice may take place with merely formal subsumption (Skillman 2013, 495). After all, an increase in labour productivity implies a drop in the labour coefficients of production, i.e. a technical change, and yields an increase of surplus value, given the working day. Hence the production of surplus value through work intensification shall be dealt with in next section.

As already observed, the theory of absolute surplus value is rather abstract, as it is based on the postulation that subsumption is only formal. Yet it is remarkable how, even at this level of analysis, Marx succeeds in laying down the building blocks of a scientific explanation of exploitation. He clarifies that exploitation is perpetrated in the production process by virtue of the workers' subordination to capitalists, but also that the production process itself is a field of class struggle and that this struggle is what ultimately determines the degree of exploitation.[4]

Besides this, Marx considers some "hybrid forms"[5] of exploitation in which "surplus labour is not extorted by direct compulsion [and] the

---

4 See also Fine (1975, 60), Lebowitz (2003, 74, 102, 143), Dooley (2005, 178), Okada (2014, 417–20).

5 The word *Zwitterformen* appears in *Capital*. Ben Fawkes translates it as "hybrid forms" (Marx 1976, 645), the International Publishers edition, as "intermediate

producer has not yet become formally subordinate to capital. In these forms, capital has not yet acquired a direct control over the labour process" (1976a, 645). He observes that these cases prevail in traditional handicraft and agricultural sectors, but also that, "as in the case of modern 'domestic industry', certain hybrid forms are reproduced here and there against the background of large-scale industry". Skillman (2019, 10–2) clarifies that, in Marx's theory, these forms do not imply subsumption proper. However, some scholars[6] interpret them as a kind of *hybrid subsumption*. Skillman is right, yet this notion might turn out to be useful in investigating certain modern labour relations in which capitalist exploitation takes place through homeworking or subcontracting to formally self-employed workers. In many of these cases, the main contractor or the contracting administrator maintains a certain power in determining the labour process and controlling the contractors. Benetton, a company that makes wide use of a modern form of the putting-out system, provides a typical example. In other cases, as in the capitalist exploitation of cooperatives, the workers maintain some freedom of choice in the labour process. In yet other cases, the workers are exploited by means of contracts for services in which the service buyer uses market power to appropriate surplus value. In some such cases, exploitation takes place through a mix of labour subsumption and capitalist market power.[7]

It must be observed that the capitalist control of the labour process is not a necessary condition for the *appropriation* of surplus value (Skillman 2007, 225; 2013, 490–1). In fact, it is possible that the market power resulting from ownership of financial or mercantile capital enables a business to appropriate a part of value added without having organised its production. In any case, subordination, as established by an employment contract, is a necessary condition for the *production* of surplus value in a capitalist system (Skillman 2019, 20–1). And the subsumption of labour capacities is a sufficient condition for the industrial capitalist's *appropriation* of this surplus value, as it implies that the capitalist himself is the owner of the commodities produced with the firm's competences.

---

forms" (Marx 1996, 511). *Uebergangsformen* (transitional forms) appears in the *Economic Manuscript of 1861–63*, while *Nebensformen* (accompanying forms) appears in the *Results*.
6 For instance, Murray (2000; 2004), Tomba (2009), Das (2012), Vrousalis (2018).
7 See Screpanti (2001) for an investigation of several of these forms.

3.2. The Production of Relative Surplus Value

Subsumption becomes real when the capitalist uses his control of the labour process to modify its structure, organization and technical characteristics. The capitalist's goal is always to increase the production of surplus value, and he normally tries to achieve this by raising labour productivity. Marx proposes the following example:

Working day IV: a-----b'-b------e

Now the length of the working day, e-a=12, is the same as that in example III above, but necessary labour is reduced by the interval b-b'=1, and surplus labour has increased by the same amount. Necessary labour is reduced because improvements in labour productivity have cut the labour content of any single commodity and therefore have enabled the capitalists to pay a given real wage with a lower value of labour power. The ensuing increase in surplus value is called "relative surplus value".

> The production of relative surplus value revolutionizes out and out the technical process of labour, and the composition of society. It therefore presupposes a specific mode of production, a mode which, along with its methods, means, and conditions, arises and develops itself spontaneously on the foundation afforded by the formal subjection of labour to capital. In the course of this development, the formal subjection is replaced by the real subjection of labour to capital (1996, 511).

When a capitalist employs many artisans in a factory, he does not just ask them to do the same jobs they did in their workshops, but reorganises the labour process to make them produce more than the summation of their preceding individual activities. Capitalism sets in motion *cooperation*: "When numerous labourers work together side by side, whether in one and the same process, or in different but connected processes, they are said to cooperate, or to work in cooperation" (330). Labour activity becomes social labour and, as such, yields a specific productive force: "the special productive power of the combined working day is, under all circumstances, the social productive power of labour, or the productive power of social labour" (334). The capitalist takes advantage of this new force. He pays the single workers but, having subsumed their labour capacities, he is the owner of the outcome of their productive organization.

Cooperation raises profits because labour activity has become social, quite independently of any form of technological innovation proper. Marx singles out several sources of improvement. Let me list them briefly:

1. The capitalist control over the labour process compels the workers to work efficiently, thus levelling out the natural differences in performance of the various artisans. *Socially necessary labour is imposed* in the capitalist factory.

2. When the means of production are used in common by many workers, the average capital-labour ratio may shrink, and the costs of constant capital per unit of output may lower. In other words, there may be an *economy in using the means of production*. Reductions in the organic composition of capital enable a capitalist to invest a given amount of capital in a bigger quantity of labour.

3. It is possible to benefit from *increasing returns to scale*: labour productivity rises because the scale of production expands (329). Thus, the greater the number of workers employed by a firm, the higher their average productivity is.

4. Due to cooperation, "mere social contact begets in most industries an *emulation* and a *stimulation of the animal spirits* that heightens the efficiency of each individual workman" (331), so that their productivity rises.[8]

---

[8] The modern psychology of labour has ascertained that recognition, self-realization and creativity are part of the fundamental psychological needs of workers. Marx had more than an intuition about that. What is remarkable is that he thinks a worker might strive to enjoy his working activity "as something which gives play to his bodily and mental powers", not only in a self-managed firm, but also in a capitalist company, where he is less "attracted by the nature of the work and the mode in which it is carried out" (Marx 1996, 188). On the other hand, we know that modern organizational psychology has led to the establishment of departments of human relations management in many big companies precisely with the goal of motivating workers to give their best. Empirical research based on Job Characteristics Theory has ascertained that labour activity can be moulded and organised in a capitalist firm to improve both labour productivity and the workers' "happiness" on the job (see Oerlemans and Bakker 2018).

5. A *saving in production time* may be achieved when different phases of the labour process are assigned to different workers, as when many bricklayers form a chain to move bricks from a place to another.

6. In addition, a *shortening of production time* is brought about when different operations in a labour process are assigned to different workers. In this way, different parts of a commodity may be produced at the same time.

7. In certain production processes there are *critical moments* that require the use of a consistent mass of workers, as in the fishing of herrings. The collaboration of many workers can tackle this problem.

8. Cooperation is also required when the *space dilation* of work is relevant, such as in canal building.

9. In other cases, cooperation may be used to achieve a saving of *faux frais* by means of a *space contraction* regarding work activity, such as in the transformation of extensive agriculture into intensive.

A more advanced form of cooperation, which Marx calls *manufacture*, develops with the introduction of a systematic division of labour. The labour process is reorganised by reducing it down to many simple functions, and these are assigned to different workers who are specialised in them. Even the instruments of labour are redesigned to serve the specialised labour functions. In manufacture, no commodity is produced by single workers. The organised group, the "social collective labourer", produces the commodity. Within the factory organization, "each workman becomes exclusively assigned to a partial function [...] his labour power is turned into the organ of this detail function" (343). Thus, the individual workers become "partial workers" and lose the ability to understand the overall labour process. This, however, is clearly understood by the capitalist who established the production plan: "intelligence in production expands in one direction, because it vanishes in many others" (366).

Here, Marx shows that he has a clear idea of what is known today as "team production". It is impossible to measure individual productivities in a "group of labourers", as this constitutes an indivisible organism, an "organised body of labour". Only the group productivity counts. The capitalist pays the *individual* workers; therefore, all the value produced by the "social worker" over and above the summation of individual wages is relative surplus value. This, of course, belongs to the capitalist, whose "undisputed authority" is used to organise and manage the organs of the overall mechanism. And "the productive power resulting from a combination of labourers appears to be the productive power of capital" (365).

The capitalist's authority is also used to cope with the workers' resistance. Obviously, Marx is not acquainted with the modern notion of "information asymmetries". Yet he repeatedly observes that, given the conflicting and exploitative relationships prevailing in a capitalist factory, workers continually practice some form of defiance and insubordination in order to preserve their dignity and reduce fatigue. Thence the capitalist's necessity to set up a hierarchy of controllers. This inflates costs, but is profitable so long as the productivity gains outweigh control costs.

Besides "simple cooperation" and "manufacture", an even more advanced form of the division of labour is set in motion by the use of machinery in modern *large-scale industry*, where the assembling of many complex means of production gives rise to an *automatic system of machines*. In this way capital incorporates science in technology, and labour productivity rises "to an extraordinary degree" (390).

The development of automation is not the result of an objective and neutral evolution of science and technology; rather, it is one of the most important consequences of real subsumption. Capital moulds science and technology in its effort to run the labour process with a view to increasing surplus value:

> The development of machinery takes this course only when large-scale industry attained a high level of development and all the sciences have been forced into the service of capital, and when, on the other hand, the machinery already in existence itself affords great resources. At this point, invention becomes a business, and the application of science to immediate production itself becomes a factor determining and soliciting science (Marx 1987, 89–90).

Marx's theory of the capitalist use of science has been developed, among others,[9] by Fallot (1966), who clarified some fundamental ideas: that the evolution of science is not neutral but intrinsically determined by capital; that technical progress brings about an ongoing separation of intellectual from manual work; and that it does not liberate the producers from work, but increasingly subjugates them to capital.

With large-scale industry, the role workers play in the labour process is transformed. In "simple cooperation" and in "manufacture" the individual workers and the organised "social worker" are still the subjects of labour activity, while the means of production are the objects. In large-scale industry, instead, "the automaton itself is the subject, and the workmen are merely conscious organs, coordinated with the unconscious organs of the automaton and, together with them, subordinated to the central moving power" (Marx 1996, 422). The partial worker undergoes another transformation: she becomes part of a machine system and is incorporated, like a human appendix, into a dead mechanism. Since scientific knowledge is now embodied in capital, the worker loses not only the ability to understand the whole production process, but also the very meaning of her labour activity and the control of her body.

Moreover, in this way, the machine becomes a weapon used by the "autocracy of capital" to smash the insubordination of workers, and is hence another means of raising relative surplus value. On the one hand, reducing workers to the condition of "organs of the automaton" abates their ability to resist the capitalist's control. On the other, the increase in the capital-labour ratio provokes a redundancy of labour, which contributes to lower wages.

3.3. Wage Dynamics

One way to raise the magnitude of surplus value is to cut wages, the part of output corresponding to necessary labour. Marx considers three different forms of wage payment: overtime pay, piece-wages and time-wages.

---

9   For example, El Kilombo (2010) and Nayeri (2018). Panzieri (1961) contributed to found "workerism" (a revolutionary section of the workers' movement in the 60's and the 70's) with his analysis of the way modern capitalism uses machines and technical progress in class struggle.

A pay scheme often used to increase surplus value consists in offering the workers extra pay for overtime work. Marx observes that competition between unemployed workers enables capitalists to cut the normal wages of the employed, thus compelling them to accept overtime work. Consequently, the actual working day lengthens beyond the normal one. As long as the ensuing increase in production outweighs the pay increase, there is a rise in surplus value.

Piecework pay is another device used by capitalists to raise relative surplus value. It may be applied to both individuals and groups. With this form of pay, workers are motivated to intensify their labour activity. At the same time, they are induced to exert self-discipline. Thus "the discipline enforced by the capitalist [...] become[s] practically superfluous in piece-work" (Marx 1998, 87), and companies can save on control costs. Therefore, productivity improves and costs shrink. Marx insists in observing that piecework pay modifies the form of wage, but does not alter the social substance of the employment contract. The worker's subordination and the subsumption of his labour capacities are maintained. Control of the labour process remains in the capitalist's hands.

The typical form of pay in a capitalist system is time-wages. Workers' compensation is not commensurate to any productive contribution. Since the employment contract establishes the workers' subordination to the capitalist for a certain number of hours a day, the capitalist pays for this time.

In his most abstract arguments, Marx, following Ricardo, assumes that normal wages are fixed at a (physically and historically determined) subsistence level. The "value of labour power" is determined by the reproduction costs of labour power. However, when he follows Adam Smith, and especially when he reflects on Union activity in Great Britain, Marx repeatedly makes it clear that, in practice, wages are determined institutionally and politically by class struggle and that they continually change in both the short and the long run:

> The periodical resistance on the part of the working men against a reduction of wages, and their periodical attempts at getting a rise of wages, are inseparable from the wage system [...]. The value of the labouring power is formed by two elements–the one merely physical, the other historical or social [...]. This historical or social element, entering into the value of labour, may be expanded, or contracted, or altogether

extinguished [...]. By comparing the standard wages or values of labour in different countries, and by comparing them in different historical epochs of the same country, you will find that the *value of labour* itself is not a fixed but a variable magnitude [...]. The fixation [of the rate of profit] is only settled by the continuous struggle between capital and labour, the capitalist constantly tending to reduce wages to their physical minimum, and to extend the working day to its physical maximum, while the working man constantly presses in the opposite direction (1985b, 144–6).

Wages are regulated by the bargaining powers of organised parties, the capitalists' associations and the workers' Trade Unions. The companies determine the level of employment through investment decisions and the workers react by carrying out industrial action.[10] Since the labour deal does not consist in the exchange of a commodity, but is a transaction instituting a title to command over a worker, labour productivity is determined ex-post by the exercise of the title itself, and depends on both the employer's managerial ability and the worker's resistance. Wages are determined by class struggle, not by productivity.

The theory of wage determination is expounded especially in *Capital*, volume 1, chapter 25, "The General Law of Capitalist Accumulation", and in the booklet *Value, Price and Profit*. It may be summarised as follows.

A decreasing function links profits to wages (given the technique) and an increasing function links investments to profits. During a prosperity phase in the business cycle, employment rises. This slackens the pressure of the industrial reserve army on labour supply. The workers' confidence mounts, and Trade Unions are able to enact struggles to support claims for wage increases and reductions in the working day. Prosperity favours the success of industrial action.

However, when wages increase, profits begin to shrink, thus weakening the inducement to invest. Eventually, investments dwindle, production follows suite, and a crisis erupts. "Crises are always prepared by precisely a period in which wages rise generally and the working class actually gets a larger share of that part of the annual product which is intended for consumption" (1997, 409). During a crisis,

---

10   See Screpanti (2000) for a reformulation of this theory with a model of efficiency wages.

companies dismiss workers and the industrial reserve army begins to bloat. This paves the way for wage cuts. Moreover, many unprofitable firms go bankrupt or are swallowed up by bigger companies, while those who survive are induced to scrap obsolete machines and replace them with more efficient ones. Productivity rises and wages slow down. Therefore, profits, investments and production expand and a new phase of prosperity matures.

In this theory, subsistence consumption does not determine normal wages, but only their lower limit. The workers are able to gain higher wages with their struggles both in the business cycle upswings and in its long run trend (Desai 1974, 19–20).

Marx observes that two general tendencies may characterise the wage trend in the very long run. Firstly, due to technical progress, which tends to systematically substitute labour with capital in response to workers' struggles, the industrial reserve army has a tendency to expand, the rate of exploitation to escalate, and the wage share in the national income to shrink.

Secondly, the level of real wages may tend to rise with labour productivity, although less than proportionally: "it is possible with an increasing productiveness of labour, for the price of labour power to keep on falling, and yet this fall to be accompanied by a constant growth of the mass of the labourers means of subsistence" (1996, 523). In fact, "a noticeable increase in wages presupposes a rapid growth of productive capital. The rapid growth of productive capital brings about an equally rapid growth of wealth, luxury, social wants, and social enjoyments." Therefore the enjoyments of the worker rise (1977, 216). Class struggle, even when it does not culminate in a revolution, is not useless. It may help the workers to reap at least a part of the growth of labour productivity, albeit at the cost of an increasing relative deprivation.

The theory of wage determination is part of Marx's scientific explanation of exploitation. It is evident that this is not a normative theory. As already observed, for Marx the "just" wage in a capitalist system is that fixed in the "labour market". It is determined by a class struggle between the capitalists and the workers, and neither of the two opposing classes is moved by moral considerations any more than by their material interests.

Class struggle takes place both inside and outside the factory. In the factory, the capitalists try to use their power to organise the labour process in view of raising labour productivity and hours worked, but they continually have to face the workers' resistance. Outside the factory, the workers form their "coalitions" and use these to compel the employers to grant improvements in pay, working hours and labour conditions. Class struggle decisively contributes to determine the degree of exploitation.

The State mainly intervenes in support of the capitalist interests, although it also undergoes the consequences of the class struggle itself. When the workers are strong enough to scare the dominant groups, the State tries to assuage conflict by complying with some of the workers' claims, e.g. by legally regulating the working day, minimum wages and labour conditions.

4. Values and Prices

After part 1, in which Marx develops a philosophy of "labour value", he uses this notion as a measure of surplus value and the rate of exploitation throughout the remainder of *Capital*, volume 1. Abstract labour is the substance of value, according to the labour theory of value. However, the expression "abstract labour" almost disappears outside part 1 or, rather, it appears mainly in the notion of "labour time", as it must when the labour hour is used as a unit of measurement.[1] The real scientific problem addressed by Marx in *Capital* is bringing to light the social relations of production through which surplus value is extracted. The theory of value serves to provide a measurement tool capable of highlighting those relations, and Marx believes that embodied labour has this property.

In section 1 of the present chapter, I illustrate the labour theory of value in the simplest way possible.[2] I describe an economy in which perfect competition and constant returns to scale prevail, and in which there are no scarce resources, no fixed capital, no joint production, no luxury goods, no complex labour and no growth. These simplifying hypotheses are assumed not just to make the text accessible to a broad

---

1   The expressions "abstract labour" or "labour in the abstract" appear 9 times in part 1 and only once in the rest of the book. "Labour time" appears 22 times in part 1 and 52 times in the rest of the book.
2   The reader interested in more complex and complete treatments may find them in Howard and King (1975), Steedman (1977), Roemer (1982), Flaschel (1983; 2010), Eatwell, Milgate and Newman (1990), Cogliano, Flaschel, Franke, Fröhlich and Veneziani (2018), who present different interpretations of Marx's value and exploitation theories.

readership, but also because my goal is to disclose the basic limitation of the labour theory of value. If this limitation is evident in the simplest model, there is no need to complicate the analysis. I argue that, since labour values are determined in a model of "commodity production in general", they only express the technical conditions of production. This is true even if surplus value and the value of labour power are introduced into the equations that determine labour values. In fact, changes in the distribution of value added between wages and profits do not have any consequence on the value of commodities, as long as the latter is determined by the amount of labour contained in them.

In section 2, I elucidate the determination of production prices, and argue that they provide a correct expression of the technical and social conditions of production. Moreover, they provide a transparent account of exploitation when they are reduced to quantities of labour commanded. I then propose a comparison between the labour embodied in and the labour commanded by a commodity, and show that the latter expresses any change in the degree of exploitation in a way the former is unable to.

In section 3, I tackle the transformation problem: given a double system approach, with a labour value system and a production price system, is it possible to transform the former into the latter whilst keeping the profit and exploitation rates invariant? I show that, even when some aggregate invariance postulates are validated with opportune normalization, the basic problem remains unsolved, i.e. the inability of labour values to correctly express the social relations of production in a capitalist economy. In fact, no reasonable normalization can achieve the invariance of the rate of exploitation and the rate of profit.[3]

---

3   Starting with a work by Okishio (1963), extensive debate and a wide body of mathematical literature have developed in attempts to *prove the existence* of capitalist exploitation on the ground of labour values. This approach demonstrates various forms of a Fundamental Marxian Theorem on the correspondence between the production of surplus value, measured in embodied labour, and the existence of positive profits. Yoshihara (2017) provides a good survey of the literature. I will not enter into this debate because the Fundamental Marxian Theorem and its generalizations are not so robust and, worse, they tend to reduce the theory of exploitation to a trivial tautology (Samuelson 1974, 64–6; Lippi 1974, 348; Vicarelli 1981, 131–6).

4.1. Labour Values

A use value, or useful article, [...] has value only because human labour in the abstract has been embodied or materialized in it. How, then, is the magnitude of this value to be measured? Plainly, by the quantity of the value-creating substance, the labour, contained in the article (Marx 1996, 48).

Not only *living labour*, living labour employed during the current year, enters into the exchangeable value of the total annual product, but also past labour, product of the labour of past years. Not only labour in living form, but labour in objectified form. The exchangeable value of the product = the total labour time which it contains, a part of which consists of living labour and a part of objectified labour (Marx 1989a, 153).

In other words:

$$v = l + vA \tag{1}$$

where v is the labour value of the "useful article", l the quantity of living labour contained in it, A the quantity of means of production used to produce it, and vA the labour objectified in it. The solution of equation (1) is:

$$v = l(I - A)^{-1} = l(I + A + ... A^t + ...) \tag{2}$$

Now value has been decomposed into quantities of labour used directly, l, and indirectly, $l(A + ... A^t + ...)$. The two equations may refer to an economy that produces a single good, in which case all symbols represent scalars and $I=1$. They can also be interpreted as referring to an economy producing n commodities. Just define v as a vector of labour values, I as the identity matrix, l as a vector of labour coefficients and A as an indecomposable and productive matrix of technical coefficients.

Equation (1) applies to a system of "production in general", or "simple commodity production". There are no profits and no wages. The producers earn the entire value added they produce. Moreover, this economy is in a state of reproduction equilibrium,[4] i.e. markets clear

---

4   This notion is clarified in Appendix 1.

and market prices coincide with the exchange values determined by the structure of production.

Marx uses labour values to measure exploitation. He often provides examples based on a single commodity, and defines value both in terms of embodied labour and in terms of Pounds, for instance: £590=£410+£90+£90=C+V+S, where the commodity value has been decomposed into constant capital, variable capital and surplus value. He then defines the rate of exploitation as £90/£90=(surplus labour)/(necessary labour) (1996, 221). He is convinced that money valuation is not a problem because, at least in his most abstract theorizations, he maintains that money is a real commodity (gold), so its value is determined by its labour content (Mohun and Veneziani 2017, 8). Nor does he consider problematic the fact that his examples refer to a single commodity rather than an array of them. At the highest level of abstraction, he assumes that all commodities exchange at money prices that are proportional to labour values. What is strange is that he measures exploitation in a capitalist economy using values prevailing in a non-capitalist economy.

Equation (1) can be converted into the following: $C+V+S=vAq+w_vL+(1-w_v)L=vq$, where q is a vector of gross outputs, $L=lq$ is the labour force employed, or aggregate living labour, and w_v is the unit value of labour power, or the labour embodied in a worker's consumption. Notice that, since $V+S=w_vL+(1-w_v)L=L$, *the distribution of output between the capitalists and the workers does not affect value determination*. Moreover, the relation between surplus value and necessary labour is linear, $S=(1-w_v)L$. Marx reasons precisely in this way, even in microeconomic analysis. When, in a working day of 12 hours, necessary labour is reduced from 6 to 5 hours, surplus *value* rises from 6 to 7.

One may ask: how can abstract labour be "embodied or materialised" in the value of a commodity? As I observed in chapter 1, some metaphors used by Marx convey the idea that abstract labour is the flow of a natural substance that "congeals" or "crystallises" into a value form. These metaphors seem to justify an interpretation according to which abstract labour consists of a productive activity entailing an expenditure of human energy. So, what is "materialised" in the value of a commodity seems to be the energy used in its production, or something akin to that.

However, such an interpretation is pointless, as "the value of commodities is the very opposite of the coarse materiality of their substance [...] the value of commodities has a purely social reality" (Marx 1996, 57). Thus, what gives rise to value is a *social* substance. And this might be true in two different senses.

First, the market process brings about a "law of value" that determines the exchange values prevailing in a reproduction equilibrium. The value relations among commodities are the fetishistic appearances of the social relations among their producers. Since such relations consist of the efficient employment of certain quantities of labour time, value could be considered an expression of the labour costs incurred in production. This makes sense. If "commodity production in general" is considered, as in equations (1) and (2), the higher-valued commodities are those whose production has required, directly and indirectly, the expenditure of a higher quantity of labour time.

The second sense in which value may be considered a social substance emerges as soon as we consider a capitalist economy. In this case, the social relations reflected in the value of commodities are those involving the social classes who participate in production, workers and capitalists. Value could still be considered an expression of direct and indirect labour costs. Since they pertain to a capitalist economy, the former are calculated as wage costs, the latter are reckoned by taking into account a capitalization factor. Therefore, this second sense in which value is the expression of a social substance cannot be represented by equations (1) and (2), where no wages and no capitalization appear.

4.2. Production Prices

> It is competition of capitals in different spheres, which first brings out the price of production equalizing the rates of profit (Marx 1998, 179).

> The fundamental law of capitalist competition [...], the law which regulates the general rate of profit and the so-called prices of production determined by it, rests, as we shall later see, on this difference between the value and the cost price of commodities (42).

In volumes 1 and 2 of *Capital,* Marx is already well aware that in a reproduction equilibrium, commodities exchange at production prices which differ from labour values, but only in volume 3 does he try to clarify this problem.

Whilst labour values have a natural standard, the labour hour, production prices depend on an arbitrary choice of numeraire. Therefore, to make them comparable to labour values, it might be useful to normalise them with the price of labour time. This is the approach I shall take in some of the following equations. In this way, production prices are expressed as labour commanded, a measure proposed by Adam Smith. Marx appreciates Smith's notion of "labour commanded", but he does not fully grasp his motivation for preferring it to embodied labour as a measure of value (Marx 1989a, 153), i.e. that value determination based on embodied labour is only valid in a non-capitalist economy. In fact, he also appreciates Ricardo's rejection of the notion of labour commanded.[5]

The prices of production, p, are determined as

$$p = l + (1 + r) pA \qquad (3)$$

where r is the rate of profit. Prices are expressed in labour commanded by posing the nominal wage $w_p=1$. The technical structure of production is the same as that in the economy represented by equation (1).

Equation (3) implies that wages are paid *post factum*, i.e. at the end of the working day or week or month. Marx is very clear about the fact that 'the labourer is not paid until after he has expended his labour power' (1996, 567), although, to comply with "the jargon of political economy", he "provisionally" adopts a formula, $r=S/(C+V)$, implying an advanced payment of wages.[6]

The solution of equation (3) is

$$p = l(I - (1 + r) A)^{-1} = l(I + (1 + r) A + \ldots (1 + r)^t A^t + \ldots) \qquad (4)$$

Exchange values have been decomposed into direct labour inputs, l, and indirect labour inputs, $l((1+r)A+\ldots(1+r)^t A^t+\ldots)$. The former are the current wage costs, the latter are the capitalised wage costs incurred in past investments.

---

[5] In any case, it must be recalled that Marx's theory of value is influenced more by Smith than by Ricardo (Foley 2011).
[6] See Appendix 2 for an elucidation of this problem.

It is evident that there are differences between production prices and labour values. Marx knows that, but does not understand the fundamental reason why this is so. He believes that the rate of surplus value is uniform in the labour value system and that the value/price differences arise because the profit rate is uniform in the production price system.

Now, assume the above equations refer to a one-commodity model. Thus, there is no problem of profit rate uniformity. Yet equations (2) and (4) reveal that, with $0<r<r_{max}$, it holds $p(r)>v$. As shown in figure 1, the labour commanded by one unit of commodity is greater than the labour embodied in it, and the higher the profit rate. Labour commanded is a correct expression of value in an economy in which capitalists exploit wageworkers, since it rises when exploitation rises. Instead, given the technique, the embodied labour does not change when the profit rate changes because it does not depend on the distribution of value added. In other words, a price-value divergence arises whenever production is production for profits, i.e. capitalist production. *The fundamental reason why labour values and production prices are different is not so much because the profit rate is uniform, but rather because it exists.*

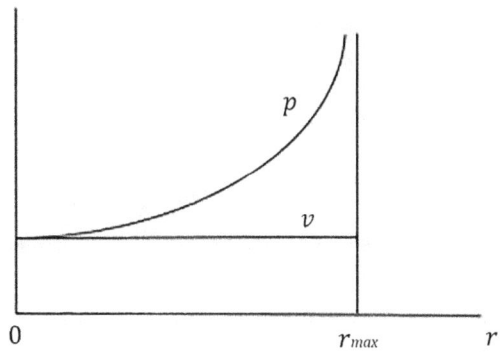

Figure 1

Let us now interpret (1)-(4) as matrix equations. They represent an economy made up of n industries and n goods. It remains true that, with $0<r<r_{max}$, it holds $p(r)>v$.[7] In any case, whatever the numeraire, $p(r)\neq v$

---

7   In fact $(I-(1+r)A)^{-1}>(I-A)^{-1}$.

holds generically.[8] The question arises: which of the two is a significant theory of value, i.e. a theory that expresses the social relations of production in a capitalist economy? The answer is immediate: only prices yield a correct valuation, for they change when the social relations of exploitation change.

Among all the possible price vectors, those normalised as labour commanded have a peculiar property: they are increasing functions of r even in the n-commodity case.[9] They are a transparent measure of value–transparent with respect to social relations–as the labours commanded by all commodities rise with exploitation, given the technique.

The rate of exploitation, measured in labour commanded, e_c, is:

$$e_c = \frac{p(I-A)q-L}{L} = \frac{l(I-(1+r)A)^{-1}(I-A)q-L}{L} = \frac{L^*}{L} \tag{5}$$

where $L^*=p(I-A)q-L$ is the quantity of labour that can be bought by surplus value.

Equation (5) measures the rate of exploitation as a ratio between two quantities of labour: that commanded by surplus value, and that commanded by the wage. Capitalists have bought power over L workers, then they have exerted power over them in the production process so as to make them produce a surplus value, which may buy power over a further amount of labour, L^*. Given the magnitude of living labour, the higher the rate of exploitation, the greater is L^*.

Rather interesting is the factor of exploitation, $1+e_c=(L+L^*)/L$, which is equal to the inverse of the wage share in net output. It is a ratio between the labour commanded by the net output and that used to produce it (Screpanti, 2003). In the presence of exploitation, this factor is greater than 1 as "the *value* of the total product can [...] buy more living labour than is contained in it" (Marx 1997, 153).

4.3. The Transformation Problem

As already observed, Marx knows very well that relative prices are different from relative labour values. Yet he maintains there is no

---

[8] Apart from when $r=0$, a special case in which the labour theory of value holds strictly $(p=v)$ is when l is an eigenvector of A (Kurz and Salvadori 1995, 110–3). This case occurs in an economy in which the organic composition of capital is uniform.

[9] The first derivatives of prices are $p'(r)=l(I-(1+r)A)^{-1}A(I-(1+r)A)^{-1}>0$.

problem in the aggregate. He thinks that abstract labour is the *substance* of value, whilst production prices only express the surface appearance of market exchanges in reproduction equilibrium, and the appearance should not alter the substance.

He seems to believe in a sort of a law of value conservation. He is confident that exchanges at production prices only redistribute value and surplus value among the different industries without altering their overall amount. He postulates that the *aggregate* value of capital and surplus value are not modified by exchanges at production prices: "The sum total of [the] cost prices of all the commodities taken together will be equal to their value [and] the total profit will be = to the total surplus value" (1989a, 415). Thus, the general rate of profit is assumed not to change when labour values are transformed into production prices. Aggregate variable capital is also supposed to be invariant (Marx 1998, 160), and this implies that not even the general rate of exploitation should change.

The aggregate invariance assumptions are expressed in various ways in different parts of *Capital*. In volume 2, they take an even stronger form. In that volume, Marx presents a two-sector model and investigates reproduction conditions in terms of the ability of the industrial system to produce the capital and consumption commodities demanded by the system itself. To define the demands and supplies of the various sectors, Marx uses both labour values and monetary prices, convinced that "the fact that prices diverge from values cannot, however, exert any influence on the movement of the social capital. On the whole, there is the same exchange of the same quantities of products, although the individual capitalists are involved in value relations no longer proportional to their respective advances and to the quantities of surplus value produced singly by every one of them" (1997, 392). When defining reproduction conditions, Marx assumes the equality of aggregate labour values and production prices, not only for the whole economy, but also for the sectorial components.[10]

Awkwardly, the aggregate invariance postulates do not hold true in the way Marx supposes, as I shall show. And this is a decisive limitation. In fact, only if the law of value conservation were correct would it be

---

10   This problem is better elucidated in Appendix 1.

possible to use the general rates of profit and exploitation, as determined in the labour value system, even when dealing with the price system.

Now, let e_v and e_p represent the rates of exploitation in labour values and production prices respectively; r_v and r_p the rates of profit in labour values and production prices respectively; $\hat{p}$ the price vector with a new normalization; w_v and w_p the unit value of labour power and the wage. And consider the following:

a) Fundamental invariance postulates

1. $e_v = e_p$

2. $r_v = r_p$

b) Subordinate invariance postulates

1. $v(I - A)q = \hat{p}(I - A)q$

2. $w_v L = w_p L$

3. $vAq = \hat{p}Aq$

Other invariance postulates can be deduced from these three. The invariance of gross output results from (b.1) and (b.3). The invariance of surplus value, from (b.1) and (b.2). I consider them *subordinate* in that they are expedient to ensuring postulates (a.1) and (a.2). These are the fundamental ones because they define the conditions that make e_v a correct measure of exploitation and r_v a correct measure of profitability, in other words, the conditions that justify Marx's practice of using e_v and r_v when dealing with the price system.

The transformation problem[11] boils down to finding a diagonal matrix D such as $vD=\hat{p}$. In general, prices are determined up to a proportionality factor. Therefore, there are many D, one for each possible numeraire, and the standard can be chosen to obtain one of the subordinate invariance postulates.

The labour value system is made up of n equations with n unknowns. Once labour values have been determined, it is sufficient to fix a bundle

---

11 See Lopes (2019) for a terse historical reconstruction of the debate on the problem.

of wage goods, g, to determine variable capital, $V=w_vL=vgL$, and the surplus value, $S=L-vgL$. There are no degrees of freedom, because labour values are determined without knowing the distributive variables. The case of the price system, in which prices depend on labour costs and the rate of profit, is different. Since social and political forces exogenously determine either w_p or r_p, the system is made up of n equations with $n+1$ unknown. There is one degree of freedom, and the possibility of introducing a normalization equation to validate one subordinate invariance postulate, but only one (Mohun and Veneziani 2017, 15).[12]

Validation of a subordinate invariance postulate does not imply validation of the fundamental ones. The rates of exploitation in the two systems are:

$$e_v = \frac{v(I-A)q - w_vL}{w_vL} \qquad (6)$$

$$e_p = \frac{p(I-A)q - w_pL}{w_pL} \qquad (7)$$

The rates of profits are:

$$r_v = \frac{v(I-A)q - w_vL}{vAq} \qquad (8)$$

$$r_p = \frac{p(I-A)q - w_pL}{pAq} \qquad (9)$$

It is easy to see that $e_v = e_p$ and $r_v = r_p$ if and only if (b.1), (b.2) and (b.3) hold, which is not the case.

Summing up, if value is a social relation, as claimed by Marx, then production prices are meaningful measures of value. This is because they convey information about both the technical and the distribution conditions of production, and change when exploitation changes.

---

[12] However, it is possible to force a further invariance postulate. If we assume that both distributive variables are unknown, i.e. that neither of them is determined exogenously, we end up with $n+2$ variables. Thence we can posit two subordinate invariance postulates and obtain, as a result, a fundamental one, but not both. For instance, by positing (b.1) and (b.2), (a.1) holds too. Loranger (2004) posits (a.2), which implies the invariance of aggregate capital and surplus value. Unsurprisingly, these devices have not met with much success among Marxist economists, as they boil down to an imaginative theory of exploitation according to which the profit rate and the wage are determined not by the social and political forces of class struggle, but by the theoretical requirements of an ingenious thinker.

Labour values, instead, respond only to changes in technical conditions. This is the reason why the rate of exploitation and the profit rate are not invariant in the transformation procedure. Now, equation 5 shows that *the actual rate of profit, r_p, is associated with the actual rate of exploitation, e_p, not with e_v. Thus, the latter is an improper measure of exploitation.*

5. Measures of Exploitation

Marx's value theory is a complex doctrine in which three different kinds of speculation coalesce: a philosophy aimed at proving that value is created by a labour substance; an explanation of the social relations of production in capitalism; and a method for measuring exploitation. My opinion is that there is no need for an essentialist philosophy to determine value, no need for a theory of value to explain capitalist social relations, and no need for a labour theory of value to measure the rate of surplus value. All we really need is a theory of production prices, possibly evaluated in labour units, as an instrument to measure exploitation. In the present chapter, I firstly bring to light some conundrums caused by using a wrong standard, then I show how to express the rate of surplus labour with a correct standard.

In section 1, I illustrate two paradoxes ensuing from the labour theory of value. One of them muddles up the explanation of technical change. In short, the labour theory of value is unable to account for the process of technical change in a capitalist economy precisely because it is a purely "technicist" theory of value. The second paradox deranges the equal exchange doctrine. This seems to be postulated by Marx to argue that fundamental capitalist exploitation occurs in the production process and not in the circulation process. Yet, if equal exchange is defined in labour values, there may be cases in which a part of surplus value emerges from the circulation process.

In section 2, I propose giving up the labour theory of value and sticking with a single system approach. Surplus value and the rate of exploitation can be measured in labour units by normalizing prices either with the wage or with labour productivity. These two kinds of normalization are consistent with each other, in the sense that they provide identical measures of the rate of exploitation and the rate of profit. However, they have different properties and can therefore be used to bring to light different aspects of the social relations of exploitation.

Finally, in section 3, I list some decisive hypotheses that are more or less implicitly assumed by Marx and the classical economists. They are decisive in that they impose severe restrictions to the theory of production prices. However, if this is only used to provide a unit of measurement, rather than a philosophy of value, such restrictions can be avoided. If they are redefined with reference to an imperfectly competitive economy, production prices can be used in empirical research to interpret the prices implicit in national account data and input-output tables as "normal" prices.

5.1. Two Paradoxes

The observation that a measure based on embodied labour gives rise to a "technicist" theory of value (Elson 1980; De Vroey 1982) is not undisputed. There are Marxists who think they can rebut it with the following proposition: the technical coefficients of production determine labour values that convey information about the way society allocates socially necessary labour among the various industries, and therefore these values do represent social relations. Such a proposition might make sense, but would not endorse the superiority of labour values. In fact, production prices convey all "social" information conveyed by them, plus that pertaining to the social relations of exploitation.

In reality, the proposition makes sense only if a single lone technique is available. If more than one exists, then the labour value system may not convey correct information on the evolution of the very technical conditions of production. This is a big problem because Marx attributes a great importance to technical progress in the theories of exploitation, capital accumulation and class struggle. Okishio (1961) proves that technical change in a capitalist economy cannot be understood by using labour values. If there is more than one technique, the price system correctly reveals which one is chosen by the capitalists, whilst use of the labour value system could lead to the wrong technique being chosen. This occurs because the profitability criterion adopted by capitalists in the choice of techniques is not based on labour productivity, and not even on the rate of surplus value or the rate of profit as determined in the labour value system. It is based on the rate of profit as determined in the price system.

The case of many techniques brings to light another reason why labour values do not convey correct information about social relations: they do not regulate the actual production conditions when technical change is motivated by profit. And this is paradoxical. Precisely because labour values only provide information on the technical conditions of production, they are unable to account for the process of technical change in a capitalist economy.

Another paradox emerges with the hypothesis of equal exchange. Marx uses the labour theory of value, among other things, to argue that capitalist exploitation takes place under apparent conditions of commutative justice, although he sometimes seems to criticise the validity of this postulation when dealing with the labour transaction. He wishes to point out that value creation is not a consequence of some asymmetry in market relations:

> If commodities, or commodities and money, of equal exchange value, and consequently equivalent, are exchanged, it is plain that no one abstracts more value from, than he throws into, circulation. There is no creation of surplus value. And in its normal form, the circulation of commodities demands the exchange of equivalents (Marx 1996, 170).

Marx intends to show that exploitation is perpetrated in the production sphere and not in the market. To this end, he seems to accept the theory that accounts for the employment relationship as if this were based on a contract of commodity exchange. Then, assuming that a worker's commodity–the use value of labour power–is traded in a competitive market, he discovers that her compensation coincides with the reproduction cost of her living labour, in other words, that the labour exchange appears to be an equal exchange. In a competitive reproduction equilibrium, transactions are supposed to be regulated by the "law of value", and "according to the law of value, exchange is between equivalents, an equal quantity of labour for an equal quantity of labour" (Marx 1989a, 213). Embodied labour determines the true value of a commodity, and transactions at true values fulfil commutative justice. When the wage coincides with the value of labour power, commutative justice ensures distributive justice too, because reproduction costs (let us say, investments in human capital) are what a worker deserves to be paid for.

Equal exchange in the "labour market", though, is a strange phenomenon. It is a real occurrence, in the sense that "production based on exchange value, on the surface of which that free and equal exchange of equivalents takes place, is basically the exchange of *objectified labour* as exchange value for living labour as use value" (1986a, 438). Yet, "from the point of view of capital, the exchange must be merely *apparent*, i.e. an economic category other than exchange, or else capital as capital and labour as labour in antithesis to it would be impossible. They would exchange for each other only as equal values" (247). They only appear to be equivalent in the circulation process.

The production sphere is the place where the fundamental capitalist misdeed is carried out. Capitalists implement production plans by using their authority. They compel workers to work efficiently and produce commodities whose value added is higher than the wage. Labour transmits to commodities a value consisting in the quantity of living labour bought by the employer. The capitalist's authority is a power of command in the production process, not a form of market power, and is what the employer actually buys with the employment contract. The acquisition of this authority implies the subsumption of labour capacities and thence the ownership of the commodities produced by them. Therefore, according to a bourgeois right, the surplus value arising from the production process legitimately belongs to the capitalist. And nobody who believes labour time is a commodity can say that the wage is unjust because it is determined in an unequal exchange.

There are two problems with this speculation. Firstly, "an equal quantity of labour" is exchanged with "an equal quantity of labour" only in a system of "commodity production in general", i.e. in a non-capitalist economy. Thus, when labour values are transformed into the production prices prevailing in a capitalist economy, a paradox may arise. In fact, since the rate of exploitation determined in the labour value system does not coincide with that determined in the price system, there could be cases in which at least a part of exploitation appears to take place in the market. To bring this oddity to light, suppose $e_v<e_p$, that is, $v((I-A)q-gL)/vgL < \breve{p}((I-A)-gL)/ \breve{p}gL$, and normalise prices, $\breve{p}$, in such a way as to yield the invariance postulate (b.2), $vgL = \breve{p}gL$. Then the wage bill in the price system coincides with the quantity of labour embodied in the workers' consumption. According to Marx (1998, 232), "from the standpoint of the total variable capital of society, the surplus value it has produced is equal to the profit it has produced". Disappointingly, this is not true. In fact, since the rate of exploitation is not affected by normalization, it happens that $e_v<e_p$ whatever the standard. Therefore it is $v((I-A)q-gL) < \breve{p}((I-A)-gL)$, which means that although the aggregate variable capital in the labour value system is identical to that prevailing in the price systems, the surplus value earned in the latter is greater than that produced in the former. Since production prices diverge from labour values to ensure market equilibrium, it is as if the surface appearance of market exchanges had yielded a surplus value over and above that produced in the labour value system. Remember that the real rate of exploitation is e_p, not e_v, and that an equal exchange postulation, defined as the exchange of "an equal quantity of labour for an equal quantity of labour", serves to argue that exploitation does not take place in the circulation process. Yet, when labour values are transformed into production prices in such a way as to ensure the invariance of variable capital, it may happen that the market generates a part of surplus value. Precisely because value is determined in the production process as embodied labour, it can be proved that there are cases in which exploitation emerges from the circulation process.

Secondly, if what capitalists buy in the "labour market" is the workers' subordination, labour time is simply a temporal limit to the obedience obligation, and cannot be considered a commodity consisting of a flow of some substance that transmits value to products. Therefore, the notion of equal exchange as an exchange of equivalent labour values portrays a situation that, rather than merely apparent, is merely fictitious.

On the other hand, Marx knows very well that wages are determined not by the crossing of demand and supply curves, but by a bargaining process. The "labour market" is not a market proper, but a battleground for class struggle. Thus, if the force that determines the rate of surplus value is not the energy of labour power, but bargaining power, what need is there of an equal exchange assumption to explain exploitation, let alone to unmask a capitalist ideology?[1]

In any case, the gist of Marx's reasoning can be upheld in a much simpler way. If one wishes to make it clear that capitalist firms may enact fundamental exploitation without resorting to any form of market power, it is sufficient to assume perfect competition in the price system. This counterfactual assumption is all that is required to argue that surplus value emerges from the production process and not from the circulation process.

5.2. A Single System Approach

A way out of the labour value impasse is to give up equation (1), and stick with equation (3) as the sole correct representation of values. The double system approach to value determination gives way to a single system approach: "There is only one economy, one system, not two. There is no 'underlying', hidden economy, which operates in values" (Duménil and Foley 2008). In other words, the only solution to the transformation problem is its dissolution.

Many Marxists, however, are unhappy with a value theory that seems to free the definitions of value and surplus value from their labour origin. Indeed, this is a serious problem for those who wish to remain faithful to a notion of abstract labour as a natural substance, as they can no longer maintain that value and surplus value are created by the energy supplied by abstract labour in the valorisation process.

Nonetheless, it is still possible to measure surplus value in labour units. It can be done in two different ways. One consists of normalizing prices with the wage and redefining them as labour commanded, as I did in chapter 4. Then surplus value becomes a quantity of labour commanded by profits, and the rate of surplus value, a ratio between two quantities of labour.

---

1   Yet the notion of "unequal exchange", as put forward by Emmanuel (1969) and developed by many students of imperialism, has turned out to be rather useful in the analysis of exploitation in international trade. Obviously, an unequal exchange situation, as revealed by the terms of trade, must be referred to a price system and not to a labour value system. See Brolin (2007) for a comprehensive survey.

The other way consists of using aggregate living labour as a standard. Sraffa (1960, 10–1) suggests this way by assuming $\breve{p}(I-A)q=1$ and $L=1$, which is tantamount to making the value of net output equal to living labour.[2] He does not mention the transformation problem. Messori (1978, 115–6), who does, proposes to normalise prices with the invariance postulate (b.1), i.e. precisely with assumption $\breve{p}(I-A)q=L$, and justifies this proposal by arguing that living labour is the sole macroeconomic variable that does not change when distribution changes.

You obtain the same result by normalizing prices with labour productivity, and this is the gist of the so-called "new interpretation". It is attributed to Duménil (1980; 1983–4) and Foley (1982); but see also Wolff, Roberts and Callari (1982) and Lipietz (1982). Following these contributions, other authors[3] have proposed reinterpretations that adopt labour productivity as a numeraire.

So, let y represent the average productivity of labour and normalise prices in this way:

$$y = \frac{\breve{p}(I-A)q}{L} = 1 \tag{10}$$

The net output is equal to the labour force employed, and one could argue that the approach boils down to a dissolution of the transformation problem that satisfies the exigency to measure prices in labour units. This looks like a re-reading, if not a re-writing, of Marx. It is not a new solution to the transformation problem. Still, it is an analytically sound solution to a philosophical problem.

With this standard, the wage share in net output becomes a share of living labour. Then the rate of exploitation can be written as

$$e_p = \frac{\breve{p}(I-A)q - w_p L}{w_p L} = \frac{L - w_p L}{w_p L} = \frac{1 - w_p}{w_p} \tag{11}$$

---

[2] Preti (2002) calls attention on the implications of such assumptions. On the ground of Sraffa's unpublished papers, Gattei (2018, 249–51) argues that this kind of numeraire is proposed by Sraffa not as "a curious object", but as a reminiscence of the Old Moor's predilection for a measure of value in labour units (see also Gattei and Gozzi, 2010, and Coveri, 2017). Mongiovi (2010) and Kurz and Salvadori (2010) have found some of Sraffa's notes that show he was interested in upholding Marx's theory of exploitation.

[3] For instance, Glick and Ehrbar (1987), Bellofiore (1989), Mohun (1994), Campbell (1997), Perri (1998), Duménil, Foley and Lévy (2009), Moseley (2016; 2017), Foley and Mohun (2016), Mohun and Veneziani (2017).

Now we can confidently say the rate of surplus value is a ratio between unpaid labour, $L-w_pL$, and paid labour, w_pL. If 1 is a working day, w_p is the part spent to produce the wage, so e_p is a ratio between the number of hours the *average* worker works for the capitalist and the number she works for herself. I say *average* because the rate of exploitation e_p holds in the aggregate, not in individual companies or industries. In fact, at a microeconomic level of analysis, value added, profits and wages are determined in terms of production prices. Microeconomic rates of exploitations, calculated in "labour time-equivalents of prices",[4] are not uniform.

To tell the truth, the new interpretation interprets itself as a "monetary" theory of labour value. In fact equation (10) can be rewritten $y=\breve{p}(I-A)q/L=1/\breve{p}_m$, where the scalar $\breve{p}_m$ is the "value of money". So, y is called "the monetary expression of value", or "the monetary expression of labour time", and represents the quantity of money corresponding to a unit of labour. The value of money, $\breve{p}_m$, also defined as the "labour expression of money", is the quantity of labour time measured by a unit of money. In the new interpretation, "labour value" is immediately represented by "money", which seems consistent with the view that the form of existence of value postulated by Marx is money, rather than labour (Key 2015).

It must also be said that a single system approach can be developed without any reference to equation (3), and a labour productivity standard can be applied to any conceivable price system (Mohun 1994, 407; Duménil and Foley 2008). Equation (3) is the one that determines prices at the highest level of abstraction compatible with that of Marx's analysis of value. At a different level of abstraction, the labour productivity standard could be applied to a fix-price oligopolistic economy with differential profit rates, as better argued below. Finally, note that some new interpreters[5] define the wage without specifying the workers' consumption bundle and take the money wage as a variable,

---

4   "Labour time-equivalents of prices" are production prices normalised with y. In the new interpretation, the prices of capital goods are the "labour time-equivalents of constant capital" (Moseley 1993; Foley 2000). They consist of dated quantities of capitalised labour rather than quantities of dead labour.

5   For instance, Duménil (1984), Duménil and Levy (1991), Moseley (1999).

possibly determined by class struggle. Marx himself does so in his less abstract investigations into wage dynamics.

Several Marxists have contested the new interpretation from a methodological or a philological point of view. To mention just a few: Roemer (1990) observes that abandoning the dual system approach opens value determination to arbitrariness; Shaikh and Tonak (1994), that it turns the whole relationship between surplus value and profit on its head; Mongiovi (2002), that it redefines value in a trivial way; Fine, Lapavitsas and Saad-Filho (2004), that it wrongly assumes value to be immediately represented by money; and Petri (2015), that it adds nothing to the comprehension of what determines profits.

In any case, although methodological and philological concerns are understandable, it must be acknowledged that the new interpretation is analytically sound. Moreover, it has fostered Marxists' commitment to empirical research (Mohun 2004; Foley 2019). Among other things, it has also helped convince many Marxists that the labour theory of value can be abandoned without prejudicing the theory of exploitation.[6]

Finally, it might be interesting to compare the two ways of measuring surplus value in labour units: "labour commanded" and "the monetary expression of labour time". Recall equation (5). Then notice that, since the rate of exploitation is a pure number, it must be $e_c = e_p$, or $L^*/L = (1-w_p) L/w_p L$. The ratio between the labour commanded by surplus value and that commanded by the wage is equal to the ratio between unpaid and paid labour. Hence, one is free to use either measure, depending on which aspects of exploitation one wishes to bring to light.

With the new interpretation, aggregate surplus value can immediately be expressed as surplus labour. It is also interesting to note that, by reducing value added to living labour, the wage rate coincides with the wage share in net output. Amongst other things, normalization with labour productivity seems to reinstate the linear relation between surplus value and the wage, $S=(1-w_p)L$, which is another way of saying that the profit share, $\pi=S/L$, and the wage share, $\omega=w_p L/L$, add up to one (Gattei and Gozzi 2010). However, some caution is required: it is not possible to re-propose Marx's *microeconomic* argument–that a reduction

---

6   However, some new interpreters, like Foley (2016; 2018), preserve the labour theory of value as an instrument that can be used to account for labour allocation.

of paid labour from 6 to 5 hours in a 12-hour working day raises the surplus value of a firm from 6 to 7. With the new interpretation, the linear relation between surplus value and the wage only holds in the aggregate, and only by virtue of a normalization convention.

An advantage of the labour commanded measure, on the other hand, is its ability to convey the idea that exploitation is based on the power that capitalists exert in the labour process. Smith's notion of "command", i.e. "power to purchase", can be easily converted into Marx's notion, i.e. "power". This is because, in the "labour market", the capitalist purchases power over his workers. Valorisation can be accounted for as a process by which the exploitation of living labour in current production engenders an increase in the quantity of labour that capitalists can command in future production.[7]

Another interesting aspect of this measure is that it can be taken as expressing a worker's point of view on capitalism and its overthrow. The factor of exploitation, $1+e_c=(L+L^*)/L$, is a ratio between the labour commanded by value added and the labour embodied in it. It could also represent a comparison between the value of net output in a capitalist economy and its value in a socialist economy.[8] The labour theory of value turns out to be of some utility after all. It can be seen as a counterfactual (Screpanti 2003) implicitly used by workers in collective decision-making; when they struggle to reduce exploitation, they are fighting against capitalism. A lessening of exploitation implies a cutback in capitalist power. Exploitation would be zeroed, $L^*=0$, if commodities

---

[7] Normalization in wage units may also be useful in macroeconomic analysis. Not by chance, it was used by Keynes in *The General Theory* (1973, chapter 4). Among its properties, the following two are worth noticing: first, when the price level varies with labour costs, the wage standard turns out to be a deflator of monetary variables that works better than index numbers; second, it can be used to convert the determination of national income into the determination of employment. This latter property is also obtained with the labour productivity standard.

[8] The young Croce (2001, 50) had an intuition about this "elliptical comparison": "Does Marx offer an explanation connecting ground and consequence, or does he not rather draw a parallel between two different phenomena, by which the diversities illuminating the origins of society are set in relief?" Croce thought the labour theory of value was aimed at criticizing the capitalist extraction of surplus value. Gramsci (2007, 192) found "a grain of truth" in his notion of "elliptical comparison", which he interpreted as implying a comparison between capitalism and a future socialist system.

were exchanged at labour values, as would occur in a hypothetical socialist economy.

Finally note that, whilst reduction of the exploitation rate to a ratio between two quantities of living labour holds true only in the aggregate, its reduction to a ratio between two quantities of commanded labour holds true at the microeconomic level too.

5.3. Back to the Real World

Having proved that production prices are better than labour values as instruments to measure exploitation, I must now say that not even the classical theory of prices should be taken at face value. Marx adopts the Smithian and Ricardian model of market competition (or "perfect liberty") with all its implicit assumptions, such as no oligopoly or monopoly power, no entry and exit barriers, no product differentiation. Especially important is the assumption of flexible market prices. These are supposed to vary as increasing functions of excess demands, with produced quantities varying as increasing functions of market prices. The market adjustment process is expected to cause a gravitation around a reproduction equilibrium, yielding market clearing and profit rate uniformity. This model may perhaps be appropriate to agriculture and financial markets, but certainly not to a modern industrial economy.

Indeed, the theory of perfect competition was not even justified in Smith's times (remember his invectives against the cabals or monopolies who fix prices to squeeze the buyers). In *The Wealth of Nations*, Smith portrays an *ideal* state of "perfect liberty", which works almost as a normative principle of social organization (McNulty 1967, 397), rather than as an explanation of the real market process. Ricardo, instead, believes that the theory describes the normal functioning of markets. But did it really account for the market process in the first half of nineteenth century? After all, Marx himself observes the tendency of company size and market power to grow in the advanced capitalist countries.[9] Thus, by complying with that theory of competition, he accepts a cliché of the science of his times, but at the price of an improper level of abstraction.

---

9   Salvadori and Signorino (2010, 12–7) found some passages in Marx's works that reveal an intuition of the notions of buyers' and sellers' market and can be interpreted by resorting to Bertrand's model of duopoly.

Farjoun and Machover (1985) suggest that competitive production prices are precisely *ideal* prices. In the real world, profit rates have no tendency to converge to uniformity, and market prices, no tendency to converge to competitive prices of production.[10] This fact can be explained by the theory of "normal pricing", as developed by post-Keynesian economists. Markets are regulated by oligopolistic competition. Normal prices are fixed by applying a gross mark-up to direct costs (labour costs plus circulating capital), which are calculated by firms with a view to normal capacity utilization in the long run. The mark-up magnitudes differ across firms and industries, and reflect the diverse "degrees of monopoly", so that profit rates are not uniform.[11]

The classical economists implicitly assume another decisive hypothesis: that the market adjustment process is stable. If it were not so, production prices would be irrelevant, as market prices would not gravitate around them. Marx has more than an intuition about market instability, especially when dealing with crises (Screpanti 1984), yet when it comes to value determination, he reasons as if the gravitation process were stable. The trouble is that stability has not been proved to hold in general, neither in neoclassical equilibrium models nor in classical gravitation models. This problem does not arise with normal prices, which are sticky and tend to vary with costs rather than with excess demands, and which are production prices coinciding with market prices.

Let us now distinguish between *competitive* production prices and *oligopolistic* production prices, the latter yielding uneven rates of profit. Normal prices are *production* prices, since they are regulated by production conditions. From an analytical viewpoint, they are

---

10 See Scharfenaker and Semieniuk (2017) for a counter-argument.
11 On the consistency between Marxian and post-Keynesian economics, see Lichtenstein (2017). Cogliano, Flaschel, Franke, Fröhlich and Veneziani (2018) develop an original interpretation of Marx's theory of value and production prices and extend it to the case of differential profit rates. Shaikh (2016, 260) rejects the neoclassical notion of perfect competition and proposes that of "real competition". He explains that this works through wage cuts, increases in labour intensity, lengthening of the working day, and technical change. Then he argues that profit rates tend to roughly equalise. The point is that real competition, i.e. competition in real capitalism, is never perfect, not even in the classical sense, because there are entry and exit barriers, unequal market powers of oligopolistic companies, product differentiation, strategic behaviours, and still other phenomena that bar any tendency of profits rates to equalise.

determined by rewriting equation (3) as $p=(l+pA)U$, where U is a diagonal matrix of different mark-ups.[12] Notice that restricting input costs to circulating capital as a basis for price determination is not a simplifying hypothesis in this case, but the illustration of a usual practice of firms. Moreover, there is no need to assume constant returns to scale throughout, as is done in the equations that determine competitive production prices.[13] It is sufficient to observe that, in practice, direct costs are constant in a neighbourhood of normal capacity utilization.

The fundamental proposition argued in this book is still valid: *oligopolistic production prices* yield a correct theory of value, as they express both the technical and social conditions of production, now including the market power by which a firm may exploit consumers and the workers of other firms.

Simply put, the need to adapt Marx's theory of prices to a modern industrial economy justifies "a systematic and principled rejection of the concept of a uniform profit rate" (Farjoun 1984, 12). All Marxists should learn such a lesson. The assumption of differential profit rates within a fix-price model is, first of all, more general than the assumption of uniformity. In fact, the theory of perfect competition can be considered as a special case: the limit case in which all the degrees of monopoly are nil.

This is often assumed in order to simplify theoretical problems and prop up some strong ideological tenets; and therefore, it can be legitimately assumed with critical intentions. Marx himself assumes competition with a somewhat critical intention: the "law of value", established through the market process, brings about an "equal exchange" situation that should rule out all the explanations of exploitation based on some form of asymmetry in market power.

Yet, Marx also follows Ricardo in believing the assumption of perfect competition to be rather realistic. Wrongly so, for it does not describe

---

12 Now, even if they are postponed, wages are treated as being paid in advance because this is the way firms fix prices. See Appendix 2.

13 In spite of his observation that cooperation in the labour process may trigger increasing returns to scale, when he comes to price determination Marx postulates constant returns to scale: "Assuming all other circumstances to be equal and a certain quantity a of some commodity to cost b labour time, a quantity na of the same commodity will cost nb labour time" (Marx 1998, 185).

the real market structure and market process in a modern capitalist economy.

Normal prices do not have this flaw and correctly account for the actual working of value formation in an economy based on oligopolistic competition. Therefore, they are not only more general, but also more realistic than competitive production prices. And precisely for this reason, they work quite well in empirical research, where measurement is effected *ex post*. The conventional prices of national accounts and input-output tables can be interpreted as normal prices.[14] The rate of surplus value is calculated as a ratio between the summation of all other incomes and the wage bill. Then, if one wishes to enlighten empirical findings by measuring exploitation in labour units, it is sufficient to redefine surplus value and the wage bill by normalizing them with the wage rate or the productivity of labour.

---

14 Some researches, for instance, Ochoa (1984), Shaikh and Tonak (1994), Cockshott, Cottrell and Michaelson (1995), Cockshott and Cottrell (1997; 1998), Shaikh (1998), Tsoulfidis and Maniatis (2002), Zachariah (2006), Fröhlich (2012), have brought to light an unexpected result, namely that there is a strong correlation in many countries between the market prices implicit in input-output tables and labour values, as well as production prices. Farjoun and Machover (1983; 1985) and Schefold (2014; 2016) attempt two different theoretical accounts of this result by using the theory of stochastic processes. Several enthusiastic Marxists seized the opportunity to claim that the labour theory of value is valid as an empirical law. This view has been criticised by Petrovic (1987), Steedman and Tomkins (1998), Kliman (2002; 2004), Dìaz and Osuna (2005–6; 2007; 2009), Nitzan and Bichler (2009), Mariolis and Soklis (2010), Vaona (2014), Screpanti (2015), Veneziani (2017). A different use of input-output tables is suggested by Cogliano, Flaschel, Franke, Fröhlich and Veneziani (2018), who are sympathetic to the "new interpretation" and read the Leontief's employment multipliers as total labour costs, obviously, "insofar as input-output coefficients can be interpreted as pure quantity magnitudes"(16).

Conclusions: Rethinking Exploitation

The explanation of exploitation constitutes the core of Marx's economic theory. It is his most innovative contribution to the science of capitalism. Better than any other socialist thinker, Marx helps us understand the institutions and social relations that form the mechanisms through which capitalism extracts surplus value from the labour activity of wageworkers. However, the edifice of his theory is not devoid of some clumsiness, for example, in his account of the employment contract, as well as the notions of abstract labour and labour value.

Marx elaborates two different theories of the employment relationship. The first describes it as an agreement for the sale of a commodity, whereby workers cede the use value of labour power, i.e. a flow of living labour springing from a stock of labour power. This commodity seems to be a *natural* abstraction with the properties of a productive force. Exploitation occurs when the exchange value of labour power is lower than its value-creating capacity. In the second theory, the employment relationship is explained as a transaction establishing workers' subordination to capitalists and the subsumption of their productive capacity under capital. While the former theory is subject to criticisms of moralism, essentialism and naturalism, the latter is not, and is able to sustain a consistent and realistic account of capitalist exploitation.

This ambivalence of Marx originates from his Hegelian and Ricardian heritage, although both Hegel and Ricardo contributed in a positive way to the formation of his science. On the negative side, Hegel bequeathed to Marx a doctrine maintaining that all contracts are agreements for the exchange of "external things". Accordingly, Marx argues that the thing exchanged in the labour market is a commodity owned by workers. Ricardo bequeathed the idea that the value of a commodity is determined by the quantity of labour used to produce it. Accordingly, Marx argues that value is a form created by abstract labour.

Ricardo, however, realises that the different capital structures in the various industries cause exchange value not to coincide with embodied labour. To overcome this difficulty, Marx envisages a model of "commodity production in general" that abstracts from capitalism. In simple commodity production, exchange value coincides with embodied labour. This cannot be concrete labour, yet it must be an objective magnitude. Thus, Marx thinks it necessary to define abstract labour as a natural substance that materialises itself into the value of commodities. When it comes to capitalist production, he does not give up this view, but rather maintains that the capitalist use of labour power is none other than a flow of abstract labour. As I argued in chapters 1 and 4, this odd blend of Hegelian and Ricardian beliefs results in an essentialist philosophy of labour and an inconsistent theory of value.

Fortunately, Marx introduces a ground-breaking innovation when he theorises that the employment relationship is not based on an agreement for the exchange of a commodity, but, instead, is a relational contract. This kind of contract is used to establish capitalist power in the production process, the power to control the labour process and compel workers to produce commodities whose value is higher than the wage. Now, abstract labour is the labour time spent by a wageworker in the production process. It is not work in a trans-historical or mercantile form. Is this definition compatible with that developed at the beginning of *Capital*?

Ça dépend. Some of the notions put forward in *Capital* must be appropriately interpreted, especially the metaphor about the substance-form relationship. *Abstract labour as labour time* could be considered a "substance", but a social substance, not a natural one. It originates from the social relationship that transforms workers into wageworkers and their labour practices into the realization of the capitalists' production plans. Labour time, so defined, is time that measures what is not (Bensaïd 2002, 82)–what is not a worker's action. Yet it is time spanning an interval of the labour process in which action does take place (Postone 1993, 202)–the capitalist's action. If an action is an activity prompted by the intention to achieve a goal posited by the actor, labour activity is not a worker's action, but the implementation of a capitalist's action. In fact, labour capacities are subsumed under capital and used as the firm's competences. Thus, the labour time multiplied by the hourly wage measures not a payment for a worker's productive contribution, but only the cost undergone by a capitalist to gain the title to command for that time.

What to do, then, with the idea that abstract labour creates, forms, or posits the value of commodities? This too has to be reinterpreted. The social substance is the social relation of production that enables a capitalist firm to produce commodities whose values yield surplus value. A change in the power relations between social classes resulting in a modification of labour productivity, working day or hourly wages can be the cause of a change in production conditions. This has, as final effect, a variation in the quantity and value of produced goods. More simply, a change in the aggregate rate of exploitation, measured as a ratio between unpaid and paid labour, causes a change in the rate of surplus value, measured as a ratio between surplus value and the wage bill. Now there is indeed a causal relationship between the social substance and value, and it is an efficient cause, not a material cause. It consists of the chain of causal links between the social conditions of production and the value of output. Clearly, one can no longer say that an increase in the natural substance of abstract labour creates an increase in the magnitude of the value form. Yet one can utter, for instance, a more interesting proposition: that an increase in working day or in labour productivity causes a change in values and an increase in profits. Note that such a notion of "substance" does not convey the idea of a transcendent essence of phenomenal appearances. There is no metaphysics in this interpretation of the substance-form relationship. There is only an analysis of the causal links that connect the social conditions of labour activity to the outcome of production.

Most of Marx's propositions in parts 1 and 2 of *Capital*, volume 1, can be reinterpreted in this manner to make them scientifically sound; most, but not all. There is an abstraction procedure that cannot be complied with in any way: the assumption that isolates production from capitalist social relations. The value of capital must not be determined in a system of "commodity production in general". The relationship between the social substance and the value form, between the social conditions of production and the value of output, cannot be investigated within a model that abstracts from history and capitalist social relations.

This interpretation constitutes an alternative to the traditional one of Hegelian-Ricardian origin and makes it possible to develop an explanation of exploitation that is exempt from all the vices of the labour theory of value. Abstract labour is not just a category resulting from a procedure of logical abstraction, and least of all an outcome of the hypostatization of such a category into a natural substance. Instead, it is a concept ensuing from the observation of a real practice of capitalist firms, namely, the practice of calculating wage costs in terms of money paid per unit of labour time. Labour, as a production input, is abstract because it is reckoned independently of the workers' concrete abilities, which are used by the capitalist firm in the production process as its own competences.

A more dauntless reinterpretation is required for the theory of value. First, the labour theory of value has to be given up, as all perceptive Marxists have now recognised. To start with, it is inconsistent with the theory of production prices. More than that: it is inapt for the measurement of capitalist exploitation, simply because it determines value in a non-capitalist system. One cannot argue that labour values represent the social structure of a capitalist mode of production, whose superficial manifestations are expressed in the exchange values of commodities.

Second, even Marx's theory of production prices has to be taken with a grain of salt. Since it only holds under perfect competition, it is subject to strongly restrictive hypotheses that make it rather unrealistic. However, if it is interpreted as an instrument of measurement referring to an economy with oligopolistic competition, it works quite well in providing a snapshot of values. And it can be used in empirical research by interpreting the conventional prices appearing in national account data and input-output tables as normal prices. Nor is it necessary to abandon the method of measuring the rate of surplus value in labour units.

The interpretation I have been proposing paves the way, among other things, for a rethinking of the demystification of commodity fetishism and bourgeois ideology: a rethinking aimed at overcoming the essentialist vulgate that prevailed over the greatest part of twentieth-century Marxism. Commodity fetishism is not a simple surface manifestation of a productive structure consisting of the labour substance of value. And ideology is not the hiding of an objective truth the philosopher can attain by unveiling the abstract essence of things behind the common knowledge of ostensible phenomena. Rather, fetishism and ideology are arrays of cultural constructs that help to constitute social reality by motivating and justifying human behaviour (Amariglio and Callari 1989).

Marx's critique of the market as a realm of equality and freedom works as the deconstruction of a fundamental institution of exploitation. It calls for rejection of the economists' conception of the employment contract as a mercantile transaction:

> The sphere of circulation or *commodity exchange*, within whose boundaries the sale and purchase of labour-power goes on, is in fact a very Eden of the innate rights of man. It is the exclusive realm of Freedom, Equality, Property and Bentham. Freedom, because both buyer and seller of a commodity, let us say, of labour-power, are determined only by their own free will. They contract as free persons, who are equal before the law. Their contract is the final result in which their joint will finds a common legal expression. Equality, because each enters into relation with the other as with a simple owner of commodity, and they exchange equivalent for equivalent (Marx 1976a, 280).

The "labour market" is the place where a very mystifying form of commodity fetishism ravages. An agreement, establishing a social relation of subjugation and exploitation, is construed as a transaction of commodity exchange, worse, of "free and equal exchange". This view is so pervasive that most philosophers, politicians, and even union leaders take it as an obvious truth, as both classical and neoclassical economists do. They reify labour by focusing on the sphere of circulation, a field in which individuals interact as if they were exchanging commodities or services.[1]

---

1 In contemporary economics, there are various ways of mystifying the employment contract. One resorts to the notion of a *contract for services*, and consists in presenting wageworkers as individuals who provide services to a company on a regular basis. This form of mystification is not very convincing, because it ignores the fact that the improbable services bought by a capitalist are not specified ex ante in the

In part 2 of *Capital*, volume 1, where the employment contract is treated as an agreement regulating a transaction in the commodity called "labour power", even Marx seems to succumb to this sort of commodity fetishism. However, his theory of labour subordination and subsumption makes it clear, beyond any doubt, that what he is trying to do is to dismantle such a form of fetishism. In the market, workers *appear* as traders who sell their commodity for a wage (Baronian 2013, 8). They *look as if* they were exchanging a commodity or a service. Yet, behind the ideological construal of the circulation process, a worker turns out to be "like someone who has brought his own hide to market and now has nothing else to expect but a tanning" (Marx 1976a, 280). "The tanning of a hide" is a metaphor hinting at what happens in the production process, where workers are compelled to work hard under the capitalist's command. In this way, the labour exchange is unmasked as the legal and ideological institution by which capital coaxes workers to accept the subordination relationship as if it were a commodity exchange.

Such a kind of deconstruction, aimed at overturning bourgeois hegemony, brings to the fore an alternative class viewpoint, according to which the employment relationship is founded on capital's despotism and the production of surplus value is made possible by the exercise of this despotism in the labour process.

---

contract and, most importantly, the fact that the workers' skills are often moulded ex post by the employer. Another form of mystification consists in seeing the employment relationship as being based on a mutually advantageous *partnership agreement* constituted in the market by equal individuals. This view is prominent in the human resource management approach, according to which the employment relationship is a long-term collaboration of employers and employees who share some basic interests. Finally, a widespread form of mystification consists in presenting the employment contract as an *agency agreement*. In this case, the worker is characterised as an agent who takes on the duty to pursue a task appointed by a principal. She is allowed to act as she likes, provided she does it in the principal's interest. Thus, a wageworker is supposed to be free to choose working practices, labour organization, work rate etc., on the condition that she aims to maximise profits. The capitalist has no authority over the worker if this is his agent. Worse still, the agent has the authority to bind the principal to accept any agreements she has signed with third parties, so long as she has done it within the agency scope. A typical example of agency agreement is the mandate relationship linking a CEO of a company to its shareholders. Hard to believe, but most neoclassical, and even many heterodox economists, consider this kind of mystification more credible than that based on the contract for services.

Finally, let us come to the question of what to do with the theory of exploitation. How can we use it, having realised that abstract labour pertains to the social relations of production, rather than to the productive forces, and that it is just the labour time spent by workers in a capitalist production process, rather than a value-creating natural substance?

Marx's rejection of any ethical implication of exploitation theory is confirmed. Marxists need not and cannot use this theory to charge capitalism with a moral condemnation. Such use would require the theory to be founded on two kinds of axioms: an ethical one, establishing that the capitalist appropriation of surplus value is unjust, and a descriptive one, establishing that surplus value is created by labour.

Now, the basic problem with ethical axioms–be they Aristotelian, Lockian, Kantian, Feuerbachian etc.–is that they are all arbitrary. In spite of their aspirations to universality, they are all dependent upon the moral preferences of the philosophers who propose them. Marx and Engels would say that they are all expressions of certain class viewpoints. And it must be recalled that Marx seeks to account for capitalist exploitation by assuming equal exchange as a bourgeois moral norm holding in capitalist markets under reproduction equilibrium. Even the distribution criterion prevailing in the first phase of communism, where "the right of the producers is proportional to the labour they supply" and incomes are commensurate to the "productive capacities of the workers", is characterised by Marx (1989d, 86) as a "bourgeois right" rather than as a universal principle of justice.

More problematic still, is the descriptive axiom typically assumed to support a moral condemnation of capitalist exploitation, that is, *value is created by living labour*.[2] This is intuitively difficult to justify once it has been clarified that abstract labour is not a value-creating substance. True, an axiom is an axiom: from a logical point of view, it requires no other justification than its postulation. Nowadays many Marxists seem happy with the "new interpretation" and a normalization whereby the

---

2   Here is how Duménil (1983–4, 432–3) postulates this axiom: "To produce is to bestow a certain amount of human labour on an ensemble of products […] Only human labour is productive […] It is necessary to postulate that this identification of value with labour incorporated holds for *any* product of any ensemble of productive processes".

monetary value of aggregate output coincides with aggregate living labour. It remains true that this is a measurement convention, and therefore constitutes a rather weak foundation for a moral condemnation of capitalist exploitation. In my opinion, the reason why a labour standard should be preferred to a gold or a dollar standard in Marxist theory is not its ability to demonstrate the injustice of surplus value. It is its ability to express the worker's view of exploitation in terms of a ratio between overwork and necessary labour.

Marx develops a scientific approach to the study of capitalism with the intention of using it as a theoretical basis for political praxis. This approach embraces: (1) a criticism of the bourgeois ideology of the employment contract as a free agreement of commodity exchange, (2) an explanation of the wage relationship as a form of labour's subordination to the capitalists, (3) an explanation of labour exploitation as a result of the exercise of capitalist power in the production process, (4) an account of modern historical evolution as a process of proletarian liberation from subordination and exploitation.

Political praxis develops in the organization of struggles. The workers' associations thrive in building class consciousness and ideological autonomy on the grounds of criticism (1) and theories (2) and (3). Then class struggle is viewed as the political action determining the process accounted for in point (4), i.e. "communism [...] the *real* movement which abolishes the present state of things" (Marx and Engels 1976a, 49).

Point (4) is based on what could be considered a descriptive axiom defining the behaviour of the political actors: workers "*have clearly, consciously proclaimed the emancipation of labour, and the transformation of society, as their goal*" (Marx 1986b, 499). The General Secretary of the International Workingmen's Association puts this proposition forward not as a hypothesis, but as the observation of a fact that occurred in the Paris Commune. In reality, it is an interpretation of the actors' intentions in that fact. Let me call it the "axiom of liberation". It is the only axiom required by Marx's theory of history as a process of social and economic progress determined by class struggle. This axiom gives foundation to a notion of revolution as a practice of self-determination.

Marx inherited from Hegel and the young Hegelians a theory of history as a process of liberation. It is true that on some occasions he remains trapped in an idealist vision of history as a teleological process ruled by Reason. And especially in his youth, he tends to speak of liberation as the dialectical process of Humankind's march toward self-consciousness. However, when he succeeds in freeing himself from any idealist notion of freedom and autonomy, he develops a theory of history as an open process. In this theory, he sees liberation as a political practice determined by the behaviour of concrete individuals embedded in a complex set of social, cultural and institutional influences (Screpanti 2007), i.e. of workers in the advanced capitalist countries of his time.

Marx is an "organic intellectual" of the working class who takes part in the process of its emancipation. He is not only an engaged social scientist; he is also a political revolutionary. The two roles sustain each other. The politician acts as an agent of the International's members. The scientist works to lay down the theoretical basis for political action. The point in which the two roles coalesce is in the clarification of the goals of political action as the expression of the workers' aspirations. This clarification takes the form of the "axiom of liberation", which, in another statement, says: "the International is *an Association of workers having for its goals the liberation of workers by the workers themselves*" (1988d, 642). The Association's goals are the workers' aspirations transformed into a political program. They are realised in "the *Commune, the political form of the social emancipation* [...]. The Commune [...] represents the liberation of 'labour', that is the fundamental and natural condition of individual and social life [...] It begins the emancipation of labour, its great goal" (1986b, 491).

Emancipation from what? "From the usurpation of the (slaveholding) monopolists of the means of labour" (490). Workers have direct experience of their own subjection to capital, because within the labour process they are subordinate to the capitalists' power and have no freedom of choice. When they achieve ideological autonomy and develop a class consciousness about their condition of oppression, they struggle for liberation.

Workers fight to expand their freedom of choice. They do so when they demand wage increases, working day reductions, extensions of social rights etc. (Screpanti 2004). And they do so when they finally struggle for communism, i.e. "to make individual property a truth by transforming the means of production, land and capital, now chiefly means of enslaving and exploiting labour, into mere instruments of *free* and associated labour" (Marx 1986b, 235) — in other words, to achieve "the self-government of the producers" (332).

Note that Marx declares workers to be moved by the goal of abolishing the conditions, not only of their enslavement, but also of their exploitation. This gives us a clue in understanding the use of exploitation theory. In Marx's approach, such a theory is an interpretation of the workers' sentiments, rather than the postulation of a philosopher's ethical principles. The workers who feel enslaved in capitalism aspire to freedom. They express this aspiration in the form of a goal of political struggle: communism. In communism, there are no capitalists and therefore no labour subjection. The sentiment of oppression is expressed by the scientist through a comparison between the workers' freedom of choice under capitalism and under communism.

On the other hand, workers feel exploited when they compare the income they earn in a capitalist production process with what they would earn in a system of "free and associated labour". Hypothesizing that they produce the same commodities with the same working hours in the two systems, they understand that their income would be higher in the latter than in the former. Alternatively, they gauge that under communism they would earn the same income they earn under capitalism but would work less. Thus, they realise that, under capitalism, they work more than is necessary to produce their income. In order to feel exploited they have no need to assume that value is created by their energy or any other natural substance. It is sufficient for them to think that profits would not exist in a communist or socialist society. Revolutionary workers become aware of the fact that profits emerge from their subordination to capital when they realise that they do not need to be subject to the command of a capitalist to produce goods.

For Marx (1989e, 520), the method of "scientific socialism" consists in "confining its scientific investigations to the knowledge of the social movement created by the people itself".[3] His theory of exploitation, as a value judgment, is an interpretation of the workers' sentiments.

---

3   The word "knowledge" does not appear in the International Publishers edition. The original phrase is: "'wissenschaftlicher Sozialismus' gebraucht worden nur im Gegensatz zum utopistischen Sozialismus, der neue Hirngespinste dem Volk aufheften will, statt seine Wissenschaft auf der Erkenntnis der vom Volk selbst gemachten sozialen Bewegung zu beschränken" (Marx 1959, 635–6).

As a scientific explanation, it is an instrument for transforming those sentiments into rational awareness of the social, institutional, economic and political conditions of surplus value production.

In a nutshell, the notion of exploitation rests on the idea that surplus value exists only because the capitalist system prevents workers to control the whole of output (Garegnani 2018, 24). When defining exploitation, it is not necessary to ascertain who the legitimate owner of surplus value is, nor who enjoys the commodities constituting surplus value. What really matters is clarifying that control of surplus value, of its production and its expenditure, pertains to the capitalists and not to the workers.

Then, awareness of exploitation can be expressed by a measure of the rate of surplus value that reduces it to the ratio between unpaid and paid labour or between the labour commanded by surplus value and that commanded by the wage bill. It can also be expressed by a factor of exploitation (the inverse of the wage share in national income), measured as a ratio between the labour commanded by net output in a capitalist economy, and that commanded by it (and contained in it), in a socialist or communist society. This kind of "elliptical comparison" is an expression of the political stance with which, on the one hand, workers transform their sense of oppression and exploitation into class consciousness, and on the other hand, anticipate the overthrow of capitalism.

Appendix 1: Reproduction Conditions

In volume 2 of *Capital*, Marx presents various schemes aimed at identifying the conditions of reproduction of a capitalist economy. Among other things, he provides numerical examples referring to a two-sector model, which, in the case of "simple reproduction", can be typified in the following way (Sweezy 1942, 162):

$$C_1 + V_1 + S_1 = V_1 + S_1 + V_2 + S_2$$

$$C_2 + V_2 + S_2 = C_1 + C_2$$

where C_i, V_i, S_i are the quantities of labour embodied in constant capital, variable capital and the surplus value of sector i.

To simplify, assume that each sector produces a single commodity, a consumer good (sector 1) and a capital good (sector 2). The above equations represent two conditions of equality between demand and supply. The left-hand sides are the values of supply, the right-hand sides are the values of demand. There are no net investments, and the workers' incomes, V_1 and V_2, as well as the capitalists' incomes, S_1 and S_2, are entirely spent in buying the consumer good. C_1 and C_2 are the parts of revenues spent by capitalists to replace the advances of capital.

Reproduction of the system implies:

$$C_1 = V_2 + S_2$$

meaning that the revenue spent by the first sector capitalists to buy the capital good must be equal to the income spent by the second sector workers and capitalists to buy the consumer good.

Reproduction conditions pertain to the *physical* consistency of the production structure: the two sectors must produce the quantities of commodities required to replicate production itself. Marx seems to think that, since equality of the demand and supply of a commodity can be expressed in physical terms, it does not matter whether their magnitudes are defined in labour values or in monetary prices: "the fact that prices diverge from values cannot, however, exert any influence on the movement of the social capital. On the whole, there is the same exchange of the same quantities of products" (Marx 1997, 392).

Yet demand and supply are decided in a market system where production decisions are motivated by the profit goal, and not by the aim of satisfying social needs. What is to be determined, therefore, is the set of *exchange values* that grant reproduction. In other words, reproduction conditions are about the prices that ensure the perpetuation of the technical and social structure of production. This refers to not only the reproduction of commodities, but also "the reproduction (i.e. maintenance) of the capitalist class and the working class, and thus the reproduction of the capitalist character of the entire process of production" (Marx 1997, 391). Not all values are appropriate, and certainly not labour values, as I will show in a moment.

A competitive *reproduction equilibrium* is the state of a capitalist economy in which markets clear and profit rates are uniform. It is achieved through a process in which: a) market prices and profits change in response to excess demands, b) supplies and demands of commodities change as consequences of consumption and investment decisions. The latter are driven by the capitalists' quest for high profits:

> The competition between capitalists–which is itself this movements towards equilibrium–consists here of their gradually withdrawing capital from spheres in which profit is for appreciable length of time below average, and gradually investing capital into spheres in which profit is above average (Marx 1998, 364).

It goes without saying that equilibrium can only occur by chance. Yet it represents the state of an economy toward which market prices and the actual profit rates should tend to gravitate:

> The different spheres of production […] constantly tend to an equilibrium: for, on the one hand, while each producer of a commodity is bound to produce a use value, to satisfy a particular social want, and while the extent of these wants differs quantitatively, still there exists an inner

relation which settles their proportion into a regular system [...]; and, on the other hand, the law of value of commodities ultimately determines how much of its disposable working time society can expend on each particular class of commodities (1996, 361).

The profit rate is brought about by market competition, but not determined by market forces:

> The average rate of profit sets in when there is an equilibrium of forces among the competing capitalists. Competition may establish this equilibrium but not the rate of profit which makes its appearance with this equilibrium (852).

The uniform profit rate is determined by production conditions, and works as an incentive to replace the capital advances that warrant reproduction of the industrial system. It is a measure of investment returns that induces capitalists to plan the required proportions of activity levels.

In reproduction equilibrium, commodities exchange at production prices. So, let me reshape the above equations in the following way (Screpanti 1993, 9):

$$p_1 q_1 = w l_1 q_1 + w l_2 q_2 + p_2(a_{21} q_1 + a_{22} q_2) r \tag{A1}$$

$$p_2 q_2 = p_2(a_{21} q_1 + a_{22} q_2) \tag{A2}$$

In this model, q_1 and q_2 are the quantities produced of the consumer and the capital goods, p_1 and p_2 are their *monetary* prices, w is the nominal wage, a_{21} and a_{22} are the technical coefficients in sectors 1 and 2, l_1 and l_2 are the labour coefficients, and r is the rate of profit. All symbols represent scalars. The left-hand sides of the two equations are the values of supplies, the right hand sides the values of demands.

It must be

$$(p_1 - w l_1 - p_2 a_{21} r) q_1 = p_2(1 - a_{22}) q_2 \tag{A3}$$

This means that the value of the consumer good not consumed by the workers and the capitalists in the consumer good sector has to be equal to the value of the capital good not consumed by the capitalists in the capital good sector.

Equations (A1) and (A2) can be rewritten

$$(p_1 - wl_1 - p_2 a_{21} r)q_1 = (wl_2 + p_2 a_{22} r)q_2$$

$$p_2(1 - a_{22})q_2 = p_2 a_{21} q_1$$

which, substituting from (A3), become

$$p_2(1 - a_{22})q_2 = (wl_2 + p_2 a_{22} r)q_2 \qquad (A1')$$

$$(p_1 - wl_1 - p_2 a_{21} r)q_1 = p_2 a_{21} q_1 \qquad (A2')$$

The two equations entail

$$1 + r = \frac{p_2 - wl_2}{p_2 a_{22}} = \frac{p_1 - wl_1}{p_2 a_{21}}$$

These are the *conditions of reproduction*. Given the wage, they determine the uniform profit rate and the production prices that ensure market clearing.

Notice that they could be obtained more directly from equation (3) of chapter 4, which, under the assumptions of this appendix, can be restyled as

$$p_1 = wl_1 + p_2 a_{21} + p_2 a_{21} r \equiv V_{p1} + C_{p1} + S_{p1}$$

$$p_2 = wl_2 + p_2 a_{22} + p_2 a_{22} r \equiv V_{p2} + C_{p2} + S_{p2}$$

where V_{pi}, C_{pi} and S_{pi} are the monetary expressions of variable capital, constant capital and surplus value in sector i.

Labour values are defined as

$$v_1 = w_v l_1 + v_2 a_{21} + (1 - w_v)l_1 \equiv V_1 + C_1 + S_1$$

$$v_2 = w_v l_2 + v_2 a_{22} + (1 - w_v)l_2 \equiv V_2 + C_2 + S_2$$

It is evident that, except in the case of a uniform organic composition of capital, conditions $V_{pi} = V_i$, $C_{pi} = C_i$, and $S_{pi} = S_i$ only occur when $r=0$, $p_1 = v_1$, $p_2 = v_2$ and $w = w_v$. When $r > 0$, conditions $p_1/p_2 \neq v_1/v_2$ and $w \neq w_v$ hold generically, and therefore $V_{pi} \neq V_i$, $C_{pi} \neq C_i$, and $S_{pi} \neq S_i$. The law of value conservation, which is not valid in the overall aggregate, a fortiori does not apply in the sectorial aggregates. In other words, reproduction conditions in a capitalist economy cannot be determined in labour values.

Appendix 2: Advanced or Postponed Wage Payments?

Marx normally defines the profit rate as $r=S/(C+V)$, which implies wages are paid in advance. Then, the matrix equation for prices is:

$$p^1 = (1 + r)wl + (1 + r)p^1 A \qquad (A4)$$

On the other hand, he declares unequivocally that

> in every country in which the capitalist mode of production reigns, it is the custom not to pay for labour power before it has been exercised for the period fixed by the contract, as for example, the end of the week. In all cases, therefore, the use value of the labour power is advanced to the capitalist: the labourer allows the buyer to consume it before he receives payment of the price; he everywhere gives credit to the capitalist (Marx 1996, 184).

In several occasions, Marx insists on the observation that "the labourer is not paid until after he has expended his labour power" (567) and that, despite the common view that "the capitalist, *using the jargon of political economy*, advances the capital laid down in wages, […] as a matter of fact the reverse takes place. It is the labourer who advances his labour to the capitalist" (1997, 219).

When wages are postponed, they are not capitalised, and the correct equation for price determination is the following:

$$p^2 = wl + (1 + r)p^2 A \qquad (A5)$$

Marx also thinks that a distorted point of view lurks behind equation (A4): "since [the capitalist] pays after the labour *has* lasted for days, weeks, or months, instead of buying it and paying for the time which it *is* to last, the whole thing amounts to a capitalist *quid pro quo*, and the advance which the labourer gives to the capitalist in labour is turned into an advance of money given to the labourer by the capitalist" (219). The "jargon of political economy" is based on such a *quid pro quo*: a blunder or misunderstanding resulting from turning one notion (advanced payment) into another (postponed payment).

Marx puts forward this criticism because he thinks the opinion that wages are advanced is an ideological deformation of reality, aimed at mystifying the social conditions of capitalist exploitation. It makes the payment of wages appear as the buying of a produced commodity, whilst, in reality, it is payment for the worker's relinquishment of his freedom and his labour capacity to the capitalist.

> What the capitalist buys is the temporary right to dispose of labour capacity, he only pays for it when this labour capacity has taken effect, objectified itself in a product. Here, as in all cases where money functions as means of payment, purchase and sale precede the real handing over of the money by the buyer. But the labour *belongs* to the capitalist after the transaction, which has been completed before the actual process of production begins. The *commodity* which emerges as product from this process belongs entirely to him. He has produced it with means of production belonging to him and with labour he has bought and which therefore belongs to him, even though it has not yet been paid for [...]. The gain that the capitalist makes, the surplus value which he realises, springs precisely from the fact that the labourer has sold to him not labour realised in a commodity, but his labour capacity itself as a commodity. If he had confronted the capitalist in the first form, as a possessor of commodities,[1] the capitalist would not have been able to make any gain, to realise any surplus labour, since according to the law of value exchange is between equivalents, an equal quantity of labour for an equal quantity of labour. The capitalist's surplus arises precisely from the fact that he buys from the labourer not a commodity but his labour capacity itself, and this has less value than the product of this labour capacity, or, what is the same thing, realises itself in more objectified labour than is realised in itself. But now, in order to justify profits, its very source is covered up, and the whole transaction from which it

---

1 According to an ideology I recalled in note 1 of the *Conclusions*, these commodities could be conceived as a series of labour services.

Appendix 2: Advanced or Postponed Wage Payments?

springs is repudiated [...]. We are now told that the labourer has sold his share in the product to the capitalist *before it has been converted into money* (1989a, 212–3).

Nonetheless, in most of his analyses, Marx defines the rate of profit as $r=S/(C+V)$. He states that, "for a clear comprehension of the relation of the parties", he "provisionally" (1996, 185) assumes the wage is advanced; and admits that, by doing so, he proceeds "according to the usual way of reckoning" (227), thus complying with "the jargon of political economy". In reality, this assumption is not so provisional.

What are the reasons for the "usual way of reckoning"? One might be that equation (A4) represents the common practice of price fixing followed by firms; normal prices are determined by applying a gross mark-up to direct costs, $C+V$. Then, as I argued in chapter 5, equation (A4) holds independently of whether wages are advanced or postponed, but simply because it corresponds to the procedure by which firms fix prices. Price fixing, however, implies that markets are not perfectly competitive. When competition is assumed–as done by Marx, following Smith and Ricardo–market prices are not fixed by firms, but are determined by the forces of demand and supply. If the market process is stable and wages are postponed, market prices must gravitate around the production prices represented by equation (A5), not equation (A4).

Another reason for the "usual way of reckoning" could be that in many sectors (e. g. agriculture), the length of the production process (one year) is longer than the length of the sub-period for wage payment (a day, a week or a month). Therefore, even if paid at the end of the day, the week or the month, wages are advanced by capitalists during the production process and thence must be capitalised at the end of the year. This observation, however, does not justify equation (A4).

In fact, suppose the annual wage, w, is post-paid in T sub-period instalments during the production process, the length of the wage payment sub-period being $1/T$ of the length of the production process. The sub-period wage is w/T. The annual factor of profit is $1+r=(1+i)^T$, where i is the sub-period rate of interest. As shown by Steedman (1977, 103–4), prices are determined as:

$$p^3 = \left[1+(1+i)+\ldots(1+i)^{T-1}\right]\frac{w}{T}l+(1+r)p^3A$$

Since $[1+(1+i)+...(1+i)^{T-1}] \cong \dfrac{(1+i)^T-1}{i} = \dfrac{r}{i}$,

it is

$$p^3 \cong \dfrac{r}{iT}wl + (1+r)p^3A \qquad (A6)$$

which is equal to (A5) when $T=1$. Now, a real economy involves production processes of different lengths. Some of them are longer than the wage payment period, while others are shorter. In abstract theory, this difficulty is overcome by assuming that all production processes, as well as the wage payment period, have the same length. Then, the question is whether (A4) or (A5) is more plausible in this idealised economy. The answer is: the most plausible is the one that better approximates equation (A6).

Steedman (1977, 105) proves that (A5) gives a good approximation for low profit rates. The degree of approximation weakens when r rises. Steedman's result can be generalised. It can be proved that equation (A5) always provides a better approximation than (A4).

Figure 2 shows the behaviour of $1+r$ and r/iT for $T=12$ and $i \in [0.001, 0.1]$. It is evident that $(1+r)-r/iT > r/iT-1$, which is the condition under which the full wage post-payment equation yields a better approximation than the full wage pre-payment equation.

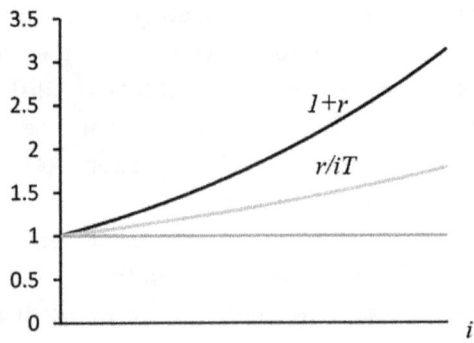

Figure 2

Appendix 2: Advanced or Postponed Wage Payments?

More generally, Lonzi, Riccarelli and Screpanti (2017) prove that

$$\left[(1+r) - \frac{r}{iT}\right] - \left(\frac{r}{iT} - 1\right) > 0, \quad \forall\, T > 0, \quad \forall\, i > 0$$

Whatever the period of wage payments and whatever the interest rates, the equation with postponed wages approximates (A6) better than the equation with advanced wages.

References

Accame, F. 2006. *Le metafore della complementarità*. Rome: Odradek.

Adler, P. S. 1990. 'Marx, Machines, and Skill.' *Technology and Culture*, 31 (4): 780–812, https://doi.org/10.2307/3105907

Ahumada, P. 2012. 'The Mercantile Form of Value and its Place in Marx's Theory of the Commodity.' *Cambridge Journal of Economics*, 36 (4): 843–67, https://doi.org/10.1093/cje/bes015

Amariglio, J. and A. Callari. 1989. 'Marxian Value Theory and the Problem of the Subject: The Role of Commodity Fetishism.' *Rethinking Marxism*, 2 (3): 31–61, https://doi.org/10.1080/08935698908657868

Arneson, R. J. 1991. 'Lockean Self-ownership: Towards a Demolition.' *Political Studies*, 39 (1): 36–54, https://doi.org/10.1111/j.1467-9248.1991.tb00580.x

Arrow, K. J. 1973. 'Some Ordinalist-Utilitarian Notes on Rawls's Theory of Justice.' *The Journal of Philosophy*, 70 (9): 245–63, https://doi.org/10.2307/2025006

Arthur, C. J. 2001. 'The Spectral Ontology of Value.' *Radical Philosophy*, 107 (May-June): 32–42.

Arthur, C. J. 2004. *The New Dialectic and Marx's 'Capital'*. Leiden: Brill.

Backhaus, H.-G. 1980. *On the Dialectics of Value-Form*. Thesis Eleven, 1 (1): 94–120.

Baronian, L. 2013. *Marx and Living Labour*. London: Routledge.

Bellofiore, R. 1989. 'A Monetary Labour Theory of Value.' *Review of Radical Political Economics*, 21 (1–2): 1–25, https://doi.org/10.1177/048661348902100103

Benhabib, S. 1984. 'Obligation, Contract and Exchange: On the Significance of Hegel's Abstract Right.' In *The State and Civil Society: Studies in Hegel's Political Philosophy*, ed. Z. A. Pelczynski. Cambridge: Cambridge University Press, 159–77.

Bensaïd, D. 2002. *Marx for Our Time*. London: Verso.

Biewener, C. 1998. 'Socially Contingent Value.' In *Marxian Economics: A Reappraisal*, vol. 2, ed. R. Bellofiore. London: Macmillan, 57–69, https://doi.org/10.1007/978-1-349-26121-5_5

Bonefeld, W. 2010. 'Abstract Labour: Against its Nature and on its Time.' *Capital and Class*, 34 (2): 257–76, https://doi.org/10.1177/0309816810367769

Bowles, S. and H. Gintis. 1988. 'Contested Exchange: Political Economy and Modern Economic Theory.' *The American Economic Review*, Papers and Proceedings, 78 (2): 145–50, https://www.jstor.org/stable/1818113

Bowles, S. and H. Gintis. 1990. 'Contested Exchange: New Microfoundations for the Political Economy of Capitalism.' *Politics and Society*, 18 (2): 165–222, https://doi.org/10.1177/003232929001800202

Braverman, H. 1974. *Labour and Monopoly Capital: The Degradation of Work in the Twentieth Century*. New York: Monthly Review Press.

Bray, J. F. 1839. *Labour's Wrongs and Labour's Remedy*. Leeds: David Green, https://archive.org/details/labourswrongsan01braygoog/page/n4

Brolin, J. 2007. *The Bias of the World: Theories of Unequal Exchange in History*. Lund: Human Ecology Division, Lund University.

Campbell, A. 1997. 'The Transformation Problem: A Simple Presentation of the New Solution.' *Review of Radical Political Economics*, 29 (3): 59–69, https://doi.org/10.1177/048661349702900307

Coase, R. H. 1937. 'The Nature of the Firm.' *Economica*, 4 (16): 386–405, https://doi.org/10.1111/j.1468-0335.1937.tb00002.x

Cockshott, W. P. and A. F. Cottrell. 1997. 'Labour Time Versus Alternative Value Bases: A Research Note.' *Cambridge Journal of Economics*, 21 (4): 545–9, https://doi.org/10.1093/oxfordjournals.cje.a013685

Cockshott, W. P. and A. F. Cottrell. 1998. 'Does Marx Need to Transform?' In *Marxian Economics: A Reappraisal*, vol. 2, ed. R. Bellofiore. Basingstoke: Macmillan, 70–85, https://doi.org/10.1007/978-1-349-26121-5_6

Cockshott, W. P., Cottrell, A. F. and G. Michaelson. 1995. 'Testing Marx: Some New Results from UK Data.' *Capital and Class*, 19 (1): 103–29, https://doi.org/10.1177/030981689505500105

Cogliano, J. F., Flaschel, P., Franke, F., Fröhlich, N. and R. Veneziani. 2018. *Value, Competition and Exploitation: Marx's Legacy Revisited*. Cheltenham: Elgar.

Cohen, G. A. 1979. 'The Labour Theory of Value and the Concept of Exploitation.' *Philosophy and Public Affairs*, 8 (4): 338–60.

Cohen, G. A. 1989. 'On the Currency of Egalitarian Justice.' *Ethics*, 99 (4): 906–44, https://doi.org/10.1086/293126

Cohen, G. A. 1995. *Self-ownership, Freedom, and Equality*. Cambridge: Cambridge University Press, https://doi.org/10.1017/CBO9780511521270

Coveri, A. 2017. 'La scuola italiana del "lavoro vivo".' XV Convegno AISPE. Verso una storia comparata del pensiero economico, Rome, November 8, http://conference.storep.org/index.php?conference=storep-annual-conferen ce&schedConf=2017&page=paper&op=viewFile&path[]=184&path[]=84

Croce, B. 2001. *Historical Materialism and the Economics of Karl Marx*. Blackmask Online, http://home.lu.lv/~ruben/Croce, Benedetto — Historical Materialism And The Economics Of Karl Marx.pdf

Das, R. 2012. 'Reconceptualizing Capitalism: Forms of Subsumption of Labour, Class Struggle, and Uneven Development.' *Review of Radical Political Economics*, 44 (2): 178–200, https://doi.org/10.1177/0486613411423895

De Angelis, M. 1995. 'Beyond the Technological and the Social Paradigms: A Political Reading of Abstract Labour as the Substance of Value.' *Capital and Class*, 19 (3): 107–34, https://doi.org/10.1177/030981689505700105

De Angelis, M. 1996. 'Social Relations, Commodity-Fetishism and Marx's Critique of Political Economy.' *Review of Radical Political Economics*, 28 (4): 1–29, https://doi.org/10.1177/048661349602800401

Desai, M. 1974. *Marxian Economic Theory*. London: Gray-Mills.

De Vroey, M. 1982. 'On the Obsolescence of the Marxian Theory of Value: A Critical Review.' *Capital and Class*, 6 (2): 34–59, https://doi.org/10.1177/030981688201700103

Dìaz, E. and R. Osuna. 2005–6. 'Can We Trust in Cross-sectional Price-Value Correlation Measures? Some Evidence from the Case of Spain.' *Journal of Post-Keynesian Economics*, 28 (2): 345–63., https://doi.org/10.2753/pke0160-3477280209

Dìaz, E. and R. Osuna. 2007. 'Indeterminacy in Price-Value Correlation Measures.' *Empirical Economics*, 33 (3): 389–99, https://doi.org/10.1007/s00181-006-0105-2

Dìaz, E. and R. Osuna. 2009. 'From Correlation to Dispersion: Geometry of the Price-Value Deviation.' *Empirical Economics*, 36 (2): 427–44, https://doi.org/10.1007/s00181-008-0203-4

Dooley, P. C. 2005. *The Labour Theory of Value*. London: Routledge.

Dowling, W. C. 1984. *Jameson, Althusser, Marx: An Introduction to 'The Political Unconscious'*. Ithaca, NY: Cornell University Press.

Duménil, G. 1980. *De la valeur aux prix de production*. Paris: Economica.

Duménil, G. 1983–4. 'Beyond the Transformation Riddle: A Labour Theory of Value.' *Science and Society*, 47 (4): 427–50.

Duménil, G. 1984. 'The So-called "Transformation Problem" Revisited: A Brief Comment.' *Journal of Economic Theory*, 33 (2): 340–8, https://doi.org/10.1016/0022-0531(84)90095-4

Duménil, G. and D. K. Foley. 2008. 'The Marxian Transformation Problem.' In *The New Palgrave*, second edition, ed. S. N. Durlauf and L. E. Blume. London: Palgrave Macmillan, http://ricardo.ecn.wfu.edu/~cottrell/ope/archive/0811/0112.html

Duménil, G., Foley, D. and D. Lévy. 2009. 'A Note on the Formal Treatment of Exploitation in a Model with Heterogenous Labour.' *Metroeconomica*, 60 (3): 560–7, https://doi.org/10.1111/j.1467-999x.2009.00353.x

Duménil, G. and D. Lévy. 1991. 'Szumski's Validation of the Labour Theory of Value: A Comment.' *Cambridge Journal of Economics*, 15 (3): 359–64, https://doi.org/10.1093/oxfordjournals.cje.a035177

Eatwell, J., Milgate, M. and P. Newman eds. 1990. *Marxian Economics*. London: Palgrave Macmillan.

Eldred, M. and M. Hanlon. 1981. 'Reconstructing Value-Form Analysis.' *Capital and Class*, 5 (1): 24–60, https://doi.org/10.1177/030981688101300103

El Kilombo. 2010. 'The Capitalist Use of Machinery: Marx Versus the Objectivists', http://www.elkilombo.org/the-capitalist-use-of-machinery-marx-versus-the-objectivists/

Ellerman, D. P. 1992. *Property and Contract in Economics: The Case for Economic Democracy*. Cambridge MA: Basil Blackwell.

Elson, D. 2015. 'The Value Theory of Labour.' In *Value: The Representation of Labour in Capitalism*, ed. D. Elson. London: Verso, 115–80.

Elster, J. 1985. *Making Sense of Marx*. Cambridge: Cambridge University Press.

Emmanuel, A. 1969. *L'échange inégal*. Paris: Maspero.

Engels, F. 1987. 'Antidühring: Herrn Eugen Dühring's Revolution in Science.' In *Collected Works*, vol. 25, by K. Marx and F. Engels. New York: International Publishers, 2001.

Engels, F. 1988. The 'Housing Question.' In *Collected Works*, vol. 23, by K. Marx and F. Engels. New York: International Publishers, 2001.

Engels, F. 1990. 'Ludwig Feuerbach and the End of the Classical German Philosophy.' In *Collected Works*, vol. 26, by K. Marx and F. Engels. New York: International Publishers, 2001.

Engelskirchen, H. 2007a. 'On the Clear Comprehension of Political Economy: Social Kinds and the Significance of Section 2 of Marx's Capital.' In *Revitalizing Causality: Realism About Causality in Philosophy and Social Science*, ed. R. Groff. London: Routledge, 242–59.

Engelskirchen, H. 2007b. 'Why is this Labour Value? Commodity-producing Labour as a Social Kind.' In *Critical Realism and the Social Sciences: Heterodox Elaborations*, ed. J. Frauley and F. Pearce. Toronto: University of Toronto Press, 202–23, https://doi.org/10.3138/9781442684232-013

Fallot, J. 1966. *Marx et le machinisme*. Paris: Cujas.

Farjoun, E. 1984. 'The Production of Commodities by Means of What?' In *Ricardo, Marx, Sraffa: The Langston Memorial Volume*, ed. E. Mandel and A. Freeman. London: Verso.

Farjoun, E. and M. Machover. 1983. *Laws of Chaos*. London: Verso.

Farjoun, E. and M. Machover. 1985. 'Probability, Economics and the Labour Theory of Value.' *New Left Review*, 152, 95–108.

Fine, B. 1975. *Marx's Capital*. London: Macmillan.

Fine, B., Lapavitsas, C. and A. Saad-Filho. 2004. 'Transforming the Transformation Problem: Why the "New Interpretation" is a Wrong Turning.' *Review of Radical Political Economics*, 36 (1): 3–19.

Finelli, R. 1987. *Astrazione e dialettica dal romanticismo al capitalismo: Saggio su Marx*. Rome: Bulzoni.

Finelli, R. 2005. *Tra moderno e postmoderno: Saggi di filosofia sociale e di etica del riconoscimento*. Lecce, Italy: Pensa Multimedia.

Flaschel, P. 1983. 'Actual Labour Values in a General Model of Production.' *Econometrica*, 51 (2): 435–54, https://doi.org/10.2307/1911999

Flaschel, P. 2010. *Topics in Classical Micro- and Macroeconomics*. New York, Springer.

Foley, D. K. 1982. 'The Value of Money, the Value of Labour Power, and the Marxian Transformation Problem.' *Review of Radical Political Economics*, 14 (2): 37–47, https://doi.org/10.1177/048661348201400204

Foley, D. K. 2000. 'Recent Developments in the Labour Theory of Value.' *Review of Radical Political Economics*, 32 (1): 1–39, https://doi.org/10.1016/s0486-6134(00)88759-8

Foley, D. K. 2011. 'The Long-period Method and Marx's Theory of Value.' In *The Evolution of Economic Theory: Essays in Honour of Bertram Schefold*, ed. V. Caspari. London: Routledge.

Foley, D. K. 2016. 'What is the Labor Theory of Value and What is it Good for?' In *Economic Theory and its History: Essays in Honour of Neri Salvadori*, eds. G. Freni, H. D. Kurz, A. M. Lavezzi, and R. Signorino. London: Routledge.

Foley, D. K. 2019. 'The "New Interpretation" After 35 Years.' Forthcoming in *Review of Radical Political Economics*.

Foley, D. K. and S. Mohun. 2016. 'Value and Price.' In *Handbook on the History of Economic Analysis*, vol. 3, 589–610. Cheltenham: Elgar, https://doi.org/10.4337/9781785365065.00046

Fracchia, J. 1995. 'Review of "Time, Labour, and Social Domination: A Reinterpretation of Marx's Critical Theory" by M. Postone.' *History and Theory*, 34 (4): 355–71, https://doi.org/10.2307/2505407

Fröhlich, N. 2012. 'Labour Values, Prices of Production and the Missing Equalization Tendency of Profit Rates: Evidence from the German Economy.' *Cambridge Journal of Economics*, 37 (5): 1107–26, https://doi.org/10.1093/cje/bes066

Garegnani, P. 2018. 'On the Labour Theory of Value in Marx and in the Marxist Tradition.' *Review of Political Economy*, 30 (4): 618–42, https://doi.org/10.1080/09538259.2018.1509546

Gattei, G. 2018, 'Pierino e il suo lupo: Come fu che Piero Sraffa chiuse in gabbia il "lupo marxicano", ma lasciandoci la chiave per ridargli la libertà.' *Dianoia: Rivista di filosofia*, 23 (26): 237–52.

Gattei, G. and G. Gozzi. 2010. 'Sraffa come economista classico: Una congettura possibile?' *Il pensiero economico italiano*, 18 (2): 75–88.

Gehrke, C. and H. D. Kurz. 2018. 'Sraffa's Constructive and Interpretive Work, and Marx.' *Review of Political Economy*, 30 (3): 428–42.

Geras, N. 1985. 'The Controversy about Marx and Justice.' *New Left Review*, 150: 47–85.

Gill, M. L. 1989. *Aristotle on Substance*. Princeton: Princeton University Press.

Glick, M. and H. Ehrbar. 1987. 'The Transformation Problem: An Obituary.' *Australian Economic Papers*, 26 (49): 294–317, https://doi.org/10.1111/j.1467-8454.1987.tb00510.x

Gordon, D. 2017. *Marx: The Analytical Marxists on Freedom, Exploitation, and Justice*. London: Routledge.

Gould, C. C. 1978. *Marx's Social Ontology: Individuality and Community in Marx's Theory of Social Reality*. Cambridge MA: MIT Press.

Graeber, D. 2013. 'It Is Value that Brings Universes into Being.' *Journal of Ethnographic Theory*, 3 (2): 219–43, https://doi.org/10.14318/hau3.2.012

Gramsci, A. 2007, *Prison Notebooks*, vol. 3. New York: Columbia University Press.

Hahnel, R. 2019. 'The Question of Profits.' *Review of Radical Political Economics*, 51 (1): 129–46, https://doi.org/10.1177/0486613417709032

Haug, F. W. 2005. *Vorlesungen zur Einführung ins 'Kapital'*, 6th edition. Hamburg: Argument Verlag.

Hegel, G. W. F. 1991. *Elements of the Philosophy of Right*. Cambridge: Cambridge University Press.

Heinrich, M. 2004. 'Ambivalences of Marx's Critique of Political Economy as Obstacles for the Analysis of Contemporary Capitalism.' Contribution to the Historical Materialist Conference, London, October 10, http://www.oekonomiekritik.de/310Ambivalences.htm

Himmelweit, S. and S. Mohun. 1978. 'The Anomalies of Capital.' *Capital and Class*, 2 (3): 67–105, https://doi.org/10.1177/030981687800600104

Hodgskin, T. 1825. *Labour Defended Against the Claims of Capital*. London: The Labour Publishing Company, https://ia800602.us.archive.org/4/items/LabourDefendedAgainstTheClaimsOfCapital/Hodgskin_1825LabourDefended.pdf

Hodgskin, T. 1827. *Popular Political Economy. Four Lectures Delivered at the London Mechanics Institution*. London: Bentley, http://lf-oll.s3.amazonaws.com/titles/320/0551_Bk.pdf

Hodgson, G. M. 1998. 'Evolutionary and Competence-based Theories of the Firm.' *Journal of Economic Studies*, 25 (1): 25–56, https://doi.org/10.1108/01443589810195606

Holmstrom, N. 1977. 'Exploitation.' *Canadian Journal of Philosophy*, 7 (2): 353–69, https://doi.org/10.1080/00455091.1977.10717024

Howard, M. C. and J. E. King. 1975. *The Political Economy of Marx*. Harlow: Longman.

Husami, Z. I. 1978. 'Marx on Distributive Justice.' *Philosophy and Public Affairs*, 8 (1): 27–64.

Hussain, A. 2015. 'Misreading Marx's Theory of Value: Marx's Marginal Notes on Wagner.' In *Value: The Representation of Labour in Capitalism*, ed. D. Elson. London: Verso.

Jameson, F. 1981. *The Political Unconscious: Narrative as a Socially Symbolic Act*. London: Methuen.

Jervolino, D. 1996. *Le parole della prassi: Saggi di ermeneutica*. Naples: La Città del Sole.

Kahn-Freund, O. 1972. *Labour and the Law*. London: The Hamlyn Trust. 3rd edition P. Davies and M. Freedland eds. London: Stevens and Sons. 1983.

Key, G. 2015. 'Why Labour is the Starting Point of Capital.' In *Value: The Representation of Labour in Capitalism*, ed. D. Elson. London: Verso.

Keynes, J. M. 1973. *The General Theory of Employment, Interest and Money*. London: Macmillan.

Kicillof, A. and G. Starosta. 2007a. 'On Materiality and Social Form: A Political Critique of Rubin's Value-form Theory.' *Historical Materialism*, 15 (3): 9–43, https://doi.org/10.1163/156920607x225852

Kicillof, A. and G. Starosta. 2007b. 'Value Form and Class Struggle: A Critique of the Autonomist Theory of Value.' *Capital and Class*, 31 (2): 13–40, https://doi.org/10.1177/030981680709200102

Kincaid, J. 2005. 'A Critique of Value-form Marxism.' *Historical Materialism*, 13 (2): 85–119, https://doi.org/10.1163/1569206054127156

Kliman, A. J. 2002. 'The Law of Value and Laws of Statistics: Sectoral Values and Prices in the US Economy, 1977–97.' *Cambridge Journal of Economics*, 26 (3): 299–311, https://doi.org/10.1093/cje/26.3.299

Kliman, A. J. 2004. 'Spurious Value-Price Correlations: Some Additional Evidence and Arguments.' In *Neoliberalism in Crisis, Accumulation, and Rosa Luxemburg's Legacy*. Research in Political Economy, vol. 21, ed. P. Zarembka. Bingley, West Yorkshire: Emerald Group Publishing Limited, 223–38, https://doi.org/10.1016/s0161-7230(04)21009-4

Knights, D. and H. Willmott eds. 1990. *Labour Process Theory*. London: Macmillan, https://doi.org/10.1007/978-1-349-20466-3

Kristjanson-Gural, D. 2009. 'Poststructural Logic in Marx's Theory of Value.' *Rethinking Marxism*, 21 (1): 14–33, https://doi.org/10.1080/08935690802542358

Kurz, H. D. and N. Salvadori. 1995. *Theory of Production: A Long-Period Analysis*. Cambridge: Cambridge University Press, https://doi.org/10.1017/cbo9780511625770

Kurz, H. D. and N. Salvadori. 2010. 'Sraffa and the Labour Theory of Value.' In *Economic Theory and Economic Thought. Essays in Honour of Ian Steedman*, ed. J. Vint, J. S. Metcalfe, H. D. Kurz, N. Salvadori and P. Samuelson. London: Routledge, 189–215.

Kurz, R. 2016. *The Substance of Capital: The Life and Death of Capitalism*. London: Chronos Publications.

Laibman, D. 2015. *Value, Technical Change and Crisis: Explorations in Marxist Economic Theory*. London: Routledge, https://doi.org/10.4324/9781315489490

Lebowitz, M. A. 2003. *Beyond Capital: Marx's Political Economy of the Working Class*, 2nd edition. London: Palgrave Macmillan.

Lichtenstein, P. M. 2017. *An Introduction to Post-Keynesian and Marxian Theories of Value and Price*. London: Routledge, https://doi.org/10.4324/9781315264967

Lipietz, A. 1982. 'The So-called Transformation Problem Revisited.' *Journal of Economic Theory*, 26 (1): 59–88, https://doi.org/10.1016/0022-0531(82)90048-5

Lippi, M. 1974. 'Lavoro produttivo, costo sociale reale e sostanza del valore nel "Capitale".' *Problemi del socialismo*, 21–2: 330–60.

Lippi, M. 1979. *Value and Naturalism in Marx*. London: New Left Books.

Lonzi, M., Riccarelli, S. and E. Screpanti. 2017. 'Advanced or Postponed Wage Payments: Sraffa validates Marx.' *Quaderni del DEPS*, 756, https://www.deps.unisi.it/sites/st02/files/allegatiparagrafo/01-06-2017/756.pdf

Lopes, T. C. 2019. 'The Transformation Problem of Values into Prices: From the Law of Value to Economic Planning.' *New Proposals: Journal of Marxism and Interdisciplinary Inquiry*, 10 (1): 29–42.

Mariolis, T. and G. Soklis. 2010. 'Additive Labour Values and Prices: Evidence from the Supply and Use Tables of the French, German and Greek Economies.' *Economic Issues*, 15 (2): 87–107.

Martini, R. 1958. *'Mercennarius': Contributo allo studio dei rapporti di lavoro in diritto romano*. Milan: Giuffrè.

Marx, K. 1959. 'Konspekt von Bakunins Buch „Staatlichkeit und Anarchie".' In *Marx Engels Werke*, vol. 18. Berlin: Dietz Verlag.

Marx, K. 1975a. 'Contribution to the Critique of Hegel's Philosophy of Law. Introduction.' In *Collected Works*, vol. 3, by K. Marx and F. Engels. New York: International Publishers, 2001.

Marx, K. 1975b. 'Economic and Philosophic Manuscripts of 1844.' In *Collected Works*, vol. 3, by K. Marx and F. Engels. New York: International Publishers, 2001.

Marx, K. 1976a. *Capital*, vol. 1. London: Penguin.

Marx, K. 1976b. 'The Poverty of Philosophy.' In *Collected Works*, vol. 6, by K. Marx and F. Engels. New York: International Publishers, 2001.

Marx, K. 1977. 'Wage Labour and Capital.' In *Collected Works*, vol. 9, by K. Marx and F. Engels. New York: International Publishers, 2001.

Marx, K. 1981. *Capital*, vol. 3. London: Penguin.

Marx, K. 1983. 'Letter to Engels,' 13 January 1859. In *Collected Works*, vol. 40, by K. Marx and F. Engels. New York: International Publishers, 2001.

Marx, K. 1985a. 'Letter to Abraham Lincoln, President of the United States of America.' Daily News, 23 December. In *Collected Works*, vol. 20, by K. Marx and F. Engels. New York: International Publishers, 2001.

Marx, K. 1985b. 'Value, Price and Profit.' In *Collected Works*, vol. 20, by K. Marx and F. Engels. New York: International Publishers, 2001.

Marx, K. 1986a. 'Economic Manuscripts of 1857–58.' In *Collected Works*, vol. 28, by K. Marx and F. Engels. New York: International Publishers, 2001.

Marx, K. 1986b. 'The Civil War in France.' In *Collected Works*, vol. 22, by K. Marx and F. Engels. New York: International Publishers, 2001.

Marx, K. 1987. 'Outlines of the Critique of Political Economy.' In *Collected Works*, vol. 29, by K. Marx and F. Engels. New York: International Publishers, 2001.

Marx, K. 1988a. 'From the Preparatory Materials.' In *Collected Works*, vol. 23, by K. Marx and F. Engels. New York: International Publishers, 2001.

Marx, K. 1988b. 'Economic Manuscript of 1861–63.' In *Collected Works*, vol. 30, by K. Marx and F. Engels. New York: International Publishers, 2001.

Marx, K. 1989a. 'Economic Manuscript of 1861–63 (cont.).' In *Collected Works*, vol. 31, by K. Marx and F. Engels. New York: International Publishers, 2001.

Marx, K. 1989b. 'Economic Manuscript of 1861–63 (cont.).' In *Collected Works*, vol. 32, by K. Marx and F. Engels. New York: International Publishers, 2001.

Marx, K. 1989c. 'Marginal Notes on Adolph Wagner's "Lehrbuch der politischen Oekonomie".' In *Collected Works*, vol. 24, by K. Marx and F. Engels. New York: International Publishers, 2001.

Marx, K. 1989d. 'Critique of the Gotha Programme.' In *Collected Works*, vol. 24, by K. Marx and F. Engels. New York: International Publishers, 2001.

Marx, K. 1989e. 'Notes on Bakunin's Book "Statehood and Anarchy".' In *Collected Works*, vol. 24, by K. Marx and F. Engels. New York: International Publishers, 2001.

Marx, K. 1994. 'Results of the Direct Production Process.' In *Collected Works*, vol. 34, by K. Marx and F. Engels. New York: International Publishers, 2001.

Marx, K. 1996. 'Capital', vol. 1. In *Collected Works*, vol. 35, by K. Marx and F. Engels. New York: International Publishers, 2001.

Marx, K. 1997. 'Capital,' vol. 2. In *Collected Works*, vol. 36, by K. Marx and F. Engels. New York: International Publishers, 2001.

Marx, K. 1998. 'Capital,' vol. 3. In *Collected Works*, vol. 37, by K. Marx and F. Engels. New York: International Publishers, 2001.

Marx, K. and F. Engels. 1976. 'The German Ideology.' In *Collected Works*, vol. 5, by K. Marx and F. Engels. New York: International Publishers, 2001.

McBride, W. L. 1975. 'The Concept of Justice in Marx, Engels and Others.' *Ethics*, 85 (3): 204–18, https://doi.org/10.1086/291958

McNulty, P. 1967. 'A Note on the History of Perfect Competition.' *Journal of Political Economy*, 75 (4): 395–9, https://doi.org/10.1086/259295

Messori, M. 1978. *Sraffa e la critica dell'economia dopo Marx: Appunti per un'analisi*. Milan: Angeli.

Milios, J., Dimoulis, D. and G. Economakis. 2018. *Karl Marx and the Classics: An Essay on Value, Crises and the Capitalist Mode of Production*. London: Routledge, https://doi.org/10.4324/9781315191652

Miller, R. W. 1984. *Analysing Marx: Morality, Power and History*. Princeton: Princeton University Press.

Mohun, S. 1994. 'A Re(in)statement of the Labour Theory of Value.' *Cambridge Journal of Economics*, 18 (4): 391–412, https://doi.org/10.1093/oxfordjournals.cje.a035282

Mohun, S. 2004. 'The Labour Theory of Value as Foundation for Empirical Investigations.' *Metroeconomica*, 55 (1): 65–95, https://doi.org/10.1111/j.0026-1386.2004.00183.x

Mohun, S. and R. Veneziani. 2017. 'Value, Price, and Exploitation: The Logic of the Transformation Problem.' *Journal of Economic Surveys*, 31 (5): 1387–420, https://doi.org/10.1111/joes.12223

Mongiovi, G. 2002. 'Vulgar Economy in a Marxian Grab: A Critique of Temporal Single System Marxism.' *Review of Radical Political Economics*, 34 (4): 393–416, https://doi.org/10.1016/s0486-6134(02)00176-6

Mongiovi, G. 2010. 'Notes on Exploitation and the Theory of Value in Marxian Economics.' Contribution to the Conference "Sraffa's Production of Commodities by Means of Commodities, 1960–2010", Rome, December 2–4, http://host.uniroma3.it/eventi/sraffaconference2010/abstracts/pp_mongiovi.pdf

Moseley, F. 1993. 'Marx's Logical Method and the Transformation Problem.' In *Marx's Method in Capital: A Reexamination*, ed. F. Moseley. Atlantic Highlands N. J.: Humanities Press, 157–83.

Moseley, F. 2000. 'The New Solution to the Transformation Problem: A Sympathetic Critique.' *Review of Radical Political Economics*, 32 (2): 282–316, https://doi.org/10.1177/048661340003200205

Moseley, F. 2016. *Money and Totality: A Macro-Monetary Interpretation of Marx's Logic in Capital and the End of the "Transformation Problem"*. Leiden: Brill.

Moseley, F. 2017. 'Money and Totality: A Macro-monetary Interpretation of Marx's Logic in Capital and the End of the "Transformation Problem".' *International Journal of Political Economy*, 46 (1): 2–21, https://doi.org/10.1080/08911916.2017.1310469

Murray, P. 2000. 'Marx's "Truly Social" Labour Theory of Value: Part I, Abstract Labour in Marxian Value Theory.' *Historical Materialism*, 6 (1): 27–66, https://doi.org/10.1163/156920600100414551

Murray, P. 2004. 'The Social and Material Transformation of Production by Capital: Formal and Real Subsumption in Capital, Volume I.' In *The Constitution of Capital: Essays on Volume I of Marx's Capital*, ed. R. Bellofiore and N. Taylor. New York: Palgrave Macmillan, 243–73 https://doi.org/10.1057/9781403938640_9

Murray, P. 2016. *The Mismeasure of Wealth*. Leiden: Brill, https://doi.org/10.1163/9789004326071

Nayeri, K. 2018. 'Capitalism, Automation, and Socialism: Karl Marx on the Labour Process.' *A Journal of Ecosocialism*, June 14, http://forhumanliberation.blogspot.com/2018/06/2942-capiatlism-automation-and.html

Nitzan, G. and S. Bichler. 2009. *Capital as Power: A Study of Order and Creorder*. New York: Routledge, https://doi.org/10.4324/9780203876329

Nozick, R. 1974. *Anarchy, State, and Utopia*. New York: Basic Books.

Ochoa, E. M. 1984. 'Labour Values and Prices of Production: An Interindustry Study of the U.S. Economy, 1947–1972.' Ph.D. dissertation, New School of Social Research, New York.

Okada, M. 2014. 'A Reassessment of Marx's Thought on Labour Exchange.' *Review of Political Economy*, 26 (3): 408–25, https://doi.org/10.1080/09538259.2014.923592

Okishio, N. 1961. 'Technical Change and the Rate of Profit.' *Kobe University Economic Review*, 7: 85–99.

Okishio, N. 1963. 'A Mathematical Note on Marxian Theorems.' *Weltwirtschaftliches Archiv*, 91: 287–99.

Oerlemans, W. G. M. and A. B. Bakker. 2018. 'Motivating Job Characteristics and Happiness at Work: A Multilevel Perspective.' *Journal of Applied Psychology*, 103 (11): 1230–41, https://doi.org/10.1037/apl0000318

Panzieri, R. 1961. 'Sull'uso capitalistico delle machine nel neocapitalismo.' *Quaderni rossi*, 1: 53–72. Reprint in R. Panzieri, *La ripresa del marxismo leninismo in Italia*. Milan: Sapere, 1972.

Peffer, R. G. 1990. *Marxism, Morality, and Social Justice*. Princeton: Princeton University Press, https://doi.org/10.1515/9781400860890

Perri, S. 1998. *Prodotto netto e sovrappiù: Da Smith al marxismo analitico e alla 'new interpretation'*. Turin: Utet.

Petri, F. 2015. 'On Some Modern Reformulations of the Labour Theory of Value.' *Contributions to Political Economy*, 34 (1): 77–104, https://doi.org/10.1093/cpe/bzv003

Petrovic, P. 1987. 'The Deviation of Production Prices from Labour Values: Some Methodology and Empirical Evidence.' *Cambridge Journal of Economics*, 11 (3): 197–210, https://doi.org/10.1093/oxfordjournals.cje.a035026

Petrucciani, S. 2012. *A lezione da Marx: Nuove interpretazioni*. Rome: Manifestolibri.

Philmore, J. 1982. 'The Libertarian Case for Slavery: A Note on Nozick.' *Philosophical Forum*, 14 (1): 43–58.

Postone, M. 1978. 'Necessity, Labour, and Time: A Reinterpretation of the Marxian Critique of Capitalism.' *Social Research*, 45 (4): 739–88.

Postone, M. 1993. *Time, Labour and Social Domination: A Reinterpretation of Marx's Critical Theory*. Cambridge: Cambridge University Press, https://doi.org/10.1017/cbo9780511570926

Preti, D. 2002. 'Sraffa e il valore-lavoro in "Produzione di merci a mezzo di merci".' In *Karl Marx e la trasformazione del pluslavoro in profitto*, ed. G. Gattei. Rome: Mediaprint, 31–46.

Reiman, J. H. 1981. 'The Possibility of a Marxian Theory of Justice.' In *Marx and morality, Suppl. 7 of Canadian Journal of Philosophy*, ed. K. Nielsen and S. C. Patten, 307–22, https://doi.org/10.1080/00455091.1981.10715776

Reuten, G. 1993. 'The Difficult Labour of a Theory of Social Value: Metaphors and Systematic Dialectics at the Beginning of Marx's Capital.' In *Marx's Method in "Capital": A Reexamination*, ed. F. Moseley. Atlantic Highlands, N.J.: Humanities Press, 89–113.

Reuten, G. 2005. 'Money as Constituent of Value: The Ideal Introversive Substance and the Ideal Extroversive Form of Value in Marx's Capital.' In *Marx's Theory of Money: Modern Appraisals*, ed. F. Moseley. London: Palgrave Macmillan, 78–92.

Reuten, G. and M. Williams. 1989. *Value-Form and the State*. London: Routledge.

Robles-Bàez, M. L. 2014. 'Dialectics of Labour and Value-Form in Marx's Capital: A Reconstruction.' In *Marx's "Capital" and Hegel's "Logic": A Reexamination*, ed. F. Moseley and T. Smith. Leiden: Brill, 292–317.

Roemer, J. E. 1982. *A General Theory of Exploitation and Class*. Cambridge, Mass.: Harvard University Press.

Roemer, J. E. 1990. 'Review of Duncan K. Foley, "Understanding Capital".' *Journal of Economic Literature*, 27(4): 1727–30.

Roemer, J. E. 1994. *Egalitarian Perspectives: Essays in Philosophical Economics*. Cambridge: Cambridge University Press, https://doi.org/10.1017/cbo9780511528293

Roemer, J. E. and J. Silvestre. 1993. 'The Proportional Solution for Economies with Both Private and Public Ownership.' *Journal of Economic Theory*, 59 (2): 426–44, https://doi.org/10.1006/jeth.1993.1027

Rubin, I. I. 1972. *Essays on Marx's Theory of Value*. Detroit: Black and Red.

Salvadori, N. and R. Signorino. 2010. 'The Classical Notion of Competition Revisited.' MPRA Paper No. 24572, https://mpra.ub.uni-muenchen.de/24572/3/MPRA_paper_24572.pdf

Samuelson, P. A. 1971. 'Understanding the Marxian Notion of Exploitation: A Summary of the So-called Transformation Problem Between Marxian Values and Competitive Prices.' *Journal of Economic Literature*, 9(2): 399–431.

Samuelson, P. A. 1974. 'Insight and Detour in the Theory of Exploitation: A reply to Baumol.' *Journal of Economic Literature*, 12 (1): 62–70.

Scharfenaker, E. and G. Semieniuk. 2017. 'A Statistical Equilibrium Approach to the Distribution of Profit Rates.' *Metroeconomica*, 68 (3): 465–99, https://doi.org/10.1111/meca.12134

Schefold, B. 2014. 'Marx, the Production Function and the Old Neoclassical Equilibrium: Workable Under the Same Assumptions?' Contribution to the Conference "What have we learned on Classical Economy since Sraffa?" Paris, Nanterre, https://ideas.repec.org/p/ris/sraffa/0019.html

Schefold, B. 2016. 'Profits Equal Surplus Value on Average and the Significance of this Result for the Marxian Theory of Accumulation.' *Cambridge Journal of Economics*, 40 (1): 165–99, https://doi.org/10.1093/cje/beu077

Screpanti, E. 1984. *Equilibrio e crisi nell'economia capitalistica: Un saggio sulla dinamica marxiana*. Rome: La Nuova Italia Scientifica.

Screpanti, E. 1993. 'Sraffa After Marx: A New Interpretation.' *Review of Political Economy*, 5 (1): 1–21, https://doi.org/10.1080/09538259300000001

Screpanti, E. 1998. 'Towards a General Theory of Capitalism: Suggestions From Chapter 23 and 27.' In *Marxian Economics: A Reappraisal*, vol. 1., ed. R. Bellofiore. Basingstoke: Macmillan, 109–23, https://doi.org/10.1007/978-1-349-26118-5_7

Screpanti, E. 2000. 'Wages, Employment, and Militancy: A Simple Model and Some Empirical Tests.' *Review of Radical Political Economics*, 32 (2); 171–96, https://doi.org/10.1177/048661340003200201

Screpanti, E. 2001. *The Fundamental Institutions of Capitalism*. London: Routledge, https://doi.org/10.4324/9780203453384

Screpanti, E. 2003. 'Value and Exploitation: A Counterfactual Approach.' *Review of Political Economy*, 15 (2): 155–71, https://doi.org/10.1080/0953825032000064869

Screpanti, E. 2004. 'Freedom and Social Goods: Rethinking Marx's Theory of Communism.' *Rethinking Marxism*, 16 (2): 185–206, https://doi.org/10.1080/08935690410001676230

Screpanti, E. 2007. *Libertarian Communism: Marx, Engels and the Political Economy of Freedom*. London: Palgrave Macmillan, https://doi.org/10.1057/9780230596474

Screpanti, E. 2011a. *Marx: Dalla totalità alla moltitudine*. Pistoia: Petite Plaisance.

Screpanti, E. 2011b. 'Freedom of Choice in the Production Sphere: The Capitalist Firm and the Self-managed Firm.' *Review of Political Economy*, 23 (2): 267–79, https://doi.org/10.1080/09538259.2011.561562

Screpanti, E. 2013. 'Aporie della giustizia: Marx a lezione da Rawls.' *Micromega: Il rasoio di Occam*, January 17, http://ilrasoiodioccam-micromega.blogautore.espresso.repubblica.it/2013/01/17/aporie-della-giustizia-marx-a-lezione-da-rawls/

Screpanti, E. 2015. 'Marx's Theory of Value, the 'New Interpretation' and the 'Empirical Law of Value': A Recap Note.' *Quaderni del DEPS*, 708, https://www.deps.unisi.it/it/ricerca/pubblicazioni-deps/quaderni-deps/anno-2015-da-n704-n724/708-marxs-theory-value-new

Screpanti, E. 2017. 'Karl Marx on Wage Labour: From Natural Abstraction to Formal Subsumption.' *Rethinking Marxism*, 29 (4): 511–37, https://doi.org/10.1080/08935696.2017.1417086

Shaikh, A. M. 1998. 'The Empirical Strength of the Labour Theory of Value.' In *Marxian Economics: A Reappraisal*, vol. 2, ed. R. Bellofiore. Basingstoke: Macmillan, 225–51, https://doi.org/10.1007/978-1-349-26121-5_15

Shaikh, A. M. 2016. *Capitalism: Competition, Conflict, Crisis*. New York: Oxford University Press, https://doi.org/10.1093/acprof:oso/9780199390632.001.0001

Shaikh, A. M. and E. A. Tonak. 1994. *Measuring the Wealth of Nations: The Political Economy of National Accounts*. Cambridge: Cambridge University Press, https://doi.org/10.1017/cbo9780511528330

Shalla, V. and W. Clement. 2007. *Work in Tumultuous Times: Critical Perspectives.* Kingston, Ontario: McGill-Queen's Press.

Simon, H. 1951. 'A Formal Theory of the Employment Relationship.' *Econometrica,* 19 (3): 293–305, https://doi.org/10.2307/1906815

Skillman, G. L. 2007. 'Value Theory vs. Historical Analysis in Marx's Account of Capitalist Exploitation.' *Science and Society,* 71 (2): 203–26, https://doi.org/10.1521/siso.2007.71.2.203

Skillman, G. L. 2013. 'The Puzzle of Marx's Missing "Results": A Tale of Two Theories.' *History of Political Economy,* 45 (3): 475–504, https://doi.org/10.1215/00182702-2334767

Skillman, G. L. 2019. 'Marx's Economic Theory of Subsumption: Reclamation and Assessment.' Working paper, Department of Economics, Wesleyan University.

Sohn-Rethel, A. 1978. *Intellectual and Manual Labour: A Critique of Epistemology.* London: Macmillan.

Sraffa, P. 1960. *Production of Commodities by Means of Commodities.* Cambridge: Cambridge University Press.

Sraffa, P. 1991. *Lettere a Tania per Gramsci.* Rome: Editori Riuniti.

Starosta, G. 2008. 'The Commodity-form and the Dialectical Method: On the Structure of Marx's Exposition in Chapter 1 of Capital.' *Science and Society,* 72 (3): 295–318, https://doi.org/10.1521/siso.2008.72.3.295

Steedman, I. 1977. *Marx After Sraffa.* London: NLB.

Steedman, I. and J. Tomkins. 1998. 'On Measuring the Deviation of Prices from Values.' *Cambridge Journal of Economics,* 22 (3): 379–85, https://doi.org/10.1093/oxfordjournals.cje.a013722

Suppes, P. 1974. 'Aristotle's Concept of Matter and its Relation to Modern Concepts of Matter.' *Synthese,* 28 (1): 27–50, https://doi.org/10.1007/bf00869495

Sweezy, P. M. 1942. *The Theory of Capitalist Development.* New York: Monthly Review Press.

Thompson, P. and C. Smith eds. 2010. *Working Life: Renewing Labour Process Analysis.* London: Palgrave Macmillan.

Tomba, M. 2009. 'Historical Temporalities of Capital: An Anti-historicist Perspective.' *Historical Materialism,* 17 (4): 44–65, https://doi.org/10.1163/146544609x12537556703115

Toscano, A. 2008. 'The Open Secret of Real Abstraction.' *Rethinking Marxism,* 20 (2): 273–87, https://doi.org/10.1080/08935690801917304

Tsoulfidis, L. and T. Maniatis. 2002. 'Values, Prices of Production and Market Prices: Some More Evidence from the Greek Economy.' *Cambridge Journal of Economics*, 26 (3): 359–69, https://doi.org/10.1093/cje/26.3.359

Tucker, R. C. 1969. *The Marxian Revolutionary Idea*. New York: Norton.

Vaccarino, G. 1988. *Scienza e semantica costruttivista*. Milan: Clup.

Vaona, A. 2014. 'A Panel Data Approach to Price-Value Correlation.' *Empirical Economics*, 47 (1): 21–34, https://doi.org/10.1007/s00181-013-0733-2

Veneziani, R. 2013. 'Exploitation, Inequality and Power.' *Journal of Theoretical Politics*, 25 (4): 526–54, https://doi.org/10.1177/0951629813477275

Veneziani, R. and N. Yoshihara. 2015. 'Exploitation in Economies with Heterogeneous Preferences, Skills and Assets: An Axiomatic Approach.' *Journal of Theoretical Politics*, 27 (1): 8–33, https://doi.org/10.1177/0951629814538911

Vicarelli, S. 1981. 'Valori, prezzi e capitalismo.' In *Valore e prezzi nella teoria di Marx*, ed. R. Panizza and S. Vicarelli. Turin: Einaudi, 75–155.

Von Weizsäcker, C. C. 1971. 'Steady State Capital Theory.' In *Lecture Notes in Operation Research and Mathematical Systems. Economics, Computer Science, Information and Control*, 54. Berlin: Springer, 102, DM 16.

Von Weizsäcker, C. C. 1973. 'Modern Capital Theory and the Concept of Exploitation. *Kyklos*, 26 (2): 245–81, https://doi.org/10.1111/j.1467-6435.1973.tb01862.x

Vrousalis, N. 2013. 'Exploitation, Vulnerability, and Social Domination.' *Philosophy and Public Affairs*, 41 (2): 131–57, https://doi.org/10.1111/papa.12013

Vrousalis, N. 2018. 'Capital Without Wage-Labour: Marx's Modes of Subsumption Revisited.' *Economics and Philosophy*, 34 (3): 411–38, https://doi.org/10.1017/s0266267117000293

Weeks, J. 2010. *Capital, Exploitation and Economic Crisis*. London: Routledge, https://doi.org/10.4324/9780203828397

White, W. R. 1956. 'The Natural Law and Commutative Justice.' *The Catholic Lawyer*, 2 (1): 31–40.

Wolff, R. D., Callari, A. and B. Roberts. 1984. 'A Marxian Alternative to the Traditional Transformation Problem.' *Review of Radical Political Economics*, 16 (2–3): 115–35, https://doi.org/10.1177/048661348401600206

Wolff, R. D., Roberts B. and A. Callari. 1982. 'Marx's (not Ricardo's) 'Transformation Problem': A Radical Reconceptualization.' *History of Political Economy*, 14 (4): 564–82, https://doi.org/10.1215/00182702-14-4-564

Wood, A. W. 1972. 'The Marxian Critique of Justice.' *Philosophy and Public Affairs*, 1 (3): 244–82.

Wood, A. W. 1984. 'Justice and Class Interest.' *Philosophica*, 33 (1): 9–32.

Wright, E. O. 2000. 'Class, Exploitation, and Economic Rents: Reflections on Sorensen's "Sounder Basis".' *American Journal of Sociology*, 105 (6): 1559–71, https://doi.org/10.1086/210464

Yoshihara, N. 1998. 'Wealth, Exploitation and Labour Discipline in the Contemporary Capitalist Economy.' *Metroeconomica*, 49 (1): 23–61, https://doi.org/10.1111/1467-999x.00039

Yoshihara, N. 2017. 'A Progress Report on Marxian Economic Theory: On the Controversies in Exploitation Theory Since Okishio.' *Journal of Economic Surveys*, 31 (2): 632–59, https://doi.org/10.1111/joes.12151

Yoshihara, N. and R. Veneziani. 2009. 'Exploitation as the Unequal Exchange of Labour: An Axiomatic Approach.' *CCES Discussion Paper Series*, No. 23.

Zachariah, D. 2006. 'Labour Value and Equalisation of Profit Rates: A Multi-country Study.' *Indian Development Review*, 4 (1): 1–21.

Index

alienation 5, 32, 33, 44
Aristotle 23
   Aristotelian 6, 17, 23, 95
automation 47, 56, 57

bourgeoisie. *See* class
Bray, John F. 6

Callari, Antonio 28, 81, 93
Capital 16, 17, 20, 23, 24, 26, 31, 33, 36, 37, 41, 45, 46, 48, 51, 59, 63, 67, 71, 90, 91, 94, 101
class. *See also* alienation
   bourgeois class 50, 67, 93, 94, 95, 96, 102
      bourgeois rights 6, 7, 78, 95
   class consciousness 8, 96, 97, 99
   class struggle 8, 13, 40, 47, 48, 50, 51, 57, 58, 59, 60, 61, 73, 76, 79, 83, 96. *See also* revolution
   working class 11, 50, 59, 67, 97, 102
commodity
   commodity exchange 3, 7, 17, 18, 19, 20, 31, 32, 34, 35, 59, 77, 90, 93, 94, 96
   commodity fetishism 5, 67, 92, 93, 94
   commodity production 12, 16, 17, 18, 19, 24, 28, 29, 30, 36, 48, 49, 55, 64, 65, 67, 78, 90, 92, 101
   commodity value 21, 29, 42, 44, 66, 78, 90

communism 4, 5, 7, 95, 96, 97, 98, 99
competition
   imperfect competition
      monopoly 85, 86, 87, 97
      oligopoly 82, 85, 86, 87, 88, 92
   perfect competition 63, 80, 85, 86, 87, 92
concrete labour 9, 12, 16, 17, 19, 23, 25, 26, 28, 29, 43, 46, 90
Contribution to the Critique of Political Economy, A 18
crisis 59
Critique of the Gotha Program 8

Duménil, Gerard 80, 81, 82, 95

Economic Manuscript of 1861–63 12, 31, 36, 39, 52
Engels, Friedrich 8, 18, 95, 96
Engelskirchen, Howard 23
exploitation
   measuring exploitation 14, 66, 75, 85, 88
   theory of exploitation 4, 7, 8, 9, 11, 13, 64, 73, 81, 83, 95, 98, 99

Fallot, Jean 57
Farjoun, Emmanuel 86, 87, 88
Feuerbachian 5, 95
Fine, Ben 51, 83
Foley, Duncan K. 68, 80, 81, 82, 83
form of value. *See* value: value form

Gordon, David 47
Graeber, David 5
Grundrisse 15, 18, 34, 42

Hegel, Georg 8, 31, 32, 33, 34, 37, 89, 96
  Elements of the Philosophy of Right 32
  Hegelian 4, 5, 7, 8, 31, 89, 90, 92
  Moralität 8
  Sittlichkeit 8, 9
Heinrich, Michael 16, 28
history 5, 7, 8, 18, 29, 92, 96, 97
  Marx's theory of history 96, 97
Hodgskin, Thomas 3, 5

justice
  commutative justice 6, 7, 77, 78
  distributive justice 6, 7, 78

Kant, Immanuel 8
  Kantian 5, 95

labour theory of value. *See* value: labour theory of value
Lapavitsas, Costas 83
Lincoln, Abraham 34
Lipietz, Alain 81
Lippi, Marco 17, 28
Locke, John 3. *See also* self-ownership
  Lockian 95
Lonzi, Marco 109

Machover, Moshé 86, 88
Marginal Notes on Wagner 7
metaphor 12, 17, 25, 26, 66, 90, 94
  irreducible metaphor 25, 26
Misery of Philosophy, The 6
Mongiovi, Gary 81, 83
monopoly. *See* competition: imperfect competition: monopoly

natural law 3, 4, 5, 6
Nozick, Robert 4

Okishio, Nobuo 64, 76
oligopoly. *See* competition: imperfect competition: oligopoly

Petri, Fabio 83
Petrucciani, Stefano 5
Proudhon, Pierre-Joseph 6. *See also* socialism: scientific socialism

Rawls, John 5
  Theory of Justice, A 5
real abstraction 13, 16, 19
Results of the Direct Production Process 12, 31, 35, 36, 39, 40, 41, 46, 51, 52
revolution 8, 9, 60, 96, 97, 98. *See also* class struggle
Ricardian 3, 6, 22, 28, 29, 85, 89, 90, 92
Ricardo, David 9, 18, 22, 28, 29, 30, 58, 68, 85, 87, 89, 90, 107
  Principles of Political Economy and Taxation, On The 29
Riccarelli, Samuele 109
Roberts, Bruce 28, 81
Roemer, John 6, 63, 83

Saad-Filho, Alfredo 83
Saint-Simon, Henri de 11
  Saint-Simonian 11
Screpanti, Ernesto 5, 8, 10, 12, 16, 37, 40, 52, 59, 70, 84, 86, 88, 97, 103, 109
self-ownership 3, 4
Shaikh, Anwar M. 83, 86, 88
Skillman, Gilbert L. 36, 51, 52
slavery 4, 16, 33, 34, 38, 40
Smith, Adam 45, 58, 68, 107
  Smithian 85
  Wealth of Nations, The 85
socialism 3, 4, 6, 8, 10, 11, 84, 85, 89, 98, 99
  scientific socialism 9, 98
Sraffa, Piero 22, 81
Steedman, Ian 63, 88, 107, 108
subordination 12, 13, 31, 33, 36, 37, 38, 39, 40, 41, 42, 45, 46, 51, 52, 58, 79, 89, 94, 96, 98. *See also* subsumption
substance of value. *See* value: value substance

Index

alienation 5, 32, 33, 44
Aristotle 23
   Aristotelian 6, 17, 23, 95
automation 47, 56, 57

bourgeoisie. *See* class
Bray, John F. 6

Callari, Antonio 28, 81, 93
Capital 16, 17, 20, 23, 24, 26, 31, 33, 36, 37, 41, 45, 46, 48, 51, 59, 63, 67, 71, 90, 91, 94, 101
class. *See also* alienation
   bourgeois class 50, 67, 93, 94, 95, 96, 102
      bourgeois rights 6, 7, 78, 95
   class consciousness 8, 96, 97, 99
   class struggle 8, 13, 40, 47, 48, 50, 51, 57, 58, 59, 60, 61, 73, 76, 79, 83, 96. *See also* revolution
   working class 11, 50, 59, 67, 97, 102
commodity
   commodity exchange 3, 7, 17, 18, 19, 20, 31, 32, 34, 35, 59, 77, 90, 93, 94, 96
   commodity fetishism 5, 67, 92, 93, 94
   commodity production 12, 16, 17, 18, 19, 24, 28, 29, 30, 36, 48, 49, 55, 64, 65, 67, 78, 90, 92, 101
   commodity value 21, 29, 42, 44, 66, 78, 90

communism 4, 5, 7, 95, 96, 97, 98, 99
competition
   imperfect competition
      monopoly 85, 86, 87, 97
      oligopoly 82, 85, 86, 87, 88, 92
   perfect competition 63, 80, 85, 86, 87, 92
concrete labour 9, 12, 16, 17, 19, 23, 25, 26, 28, 29, 43, 46, 90
Contribution to the Critique of Political Economy, A 18
crisis 59
Critique of the Gotha Program 8

Duménil, Gerard 80, 81, 82, 95

Economic Manuscript of 1861–63 12, 31, 36, 39, 52
Engels, Friedrich 8, 18, 95, 96
Engelskirchen, Howard 23
exploitation
   measuring exploitation 14, 66, 75, 85, 88
   theory of exploitation 4, 7, 8, 9, 11, 13, 64, 73, 81, 83, 95, 98, 99

Fallot, Jean 57
Farjoun, Emmanuel 86, 87, 88
Feuerbachian 5, 95
Fine, Ben 51, 83
Foley, Duncan K. 68, 80, 81, 82, 83
form of value. *See* value: value form

Gordon, David 47
Graeber, David 5
Grundrisse 15, 18, 34, 42

Hegel, Georg 8, 31, 32, 33, 34, 37, 89, 96
   Elements of the Philosophy of Right 32
   Hegelian 4, 5, 7, 8, 31, 89, 90, 92
   Moralität 8
   Sittlichkeit 8, 9
Heinrich, Michael 16, 28
history 5, 7, 8, 18, 29, 92, 96, 97
   Marx's theory of history 96, 97
Hodgskin, Thomas 3, 5

justice
   commutative justice 6, 7, 77, 78
   distributive justice 6, 7, 78

Kant, Immanuel 8
   Kantian 5, 95

labour theory of value. *See* value: labour theory of value
Lapavitsas, Costas 83
Lincoln, Abraham 34
Lipietz, Alain 81
Lippi, Marco 17, 28
Locke, John 3. *See also* self-ownership
   Lockian 95
Lonzi, Marco 109

Machover, Moshé 86, 88
Marginal Notes on Wagner 7
metaphor 12, 17, 25, 26, 66, 90, 94
   irreducible metaphor 25, 26
Misery of Philosophy, The 6
Mongiovi, Gary 81, 83
monopoly. *See* competition: imperfect competition: monopoly

natural law 3, 4, 5, 6
Nozick, Robert 4

Okishio, Nobuo 64, 76
oligopoly. *See* competition: imperfect competition: oligopoly

Petri, Fabio 83
Petrucciani, Stefano 5
Proudhon, Pierre-Joseph 6. *See also* socialism: scientific socialism

Rawls, John 5
   Theory of Justice, A 5
real abstraction 13, 16, 19
Results of the Direct Production Process 12, 31, 35, 36, 39, 40, 41, 46, 51, 52
revolution 8, 9, 60, 96, 97, 98. *See also* class struggle
Ricardian 3, 6, 22, 28, 29, 85, 89, 90, 92
Ricardo, David 9, 18, 22, 28, 29, 30, 58, 68, 85, 87, 89, 90, 107
   Principles of Political Economy and Taxation, On The 29
Riccarelli, Samuele 109
Roberts, Bruce 28, 81
Roemer, John 6, 63, 83

Saad-Filho, Alfredo 83
Saint-Simon, Henri de 11
   Saint-Simonian 11
Screpanti, Ernesto 5, 8, 10, 12, 16, 37, 40, 52, 59, 70, 84, 86, 88, 97, 103, 109
self-ownership 3, 4
Shaikh, Anwar M. 83, 86, 88
Skillman, Gilbert L. 36, 51, 52
slavery 4, 16, 33, 34, 38, 40
Smith, Adam 45, 58, 68, 107
   Smithian 85
   Wealth of Nations, The 85
socialism 3, 4, 6, 8, 10, 11, 84, 85, 89, 98, 99
   scientific socialism 9, 98
Sraffa, Piero 22, 81
Steedman, Ian 63, 88, 107, 108
subordination 12, 13, 31, 33, 36, 37, 38, 39, 40, 41, 42, 45, 46, 51, 52, 58, 79, 89, 94, 96, 98. *See also* subsumption
substance of value. *See* value: value substance

subsumption 12, 13, 31, 36, 37, 38, 39, 40, 42, 45, 47, 48, 49, 51, 52, 56, 58, 78, 89, 94. *See also* subordination
surplus value. *See* value: surplus value

Thomist 6
Tonak, E. Ahmet 83, 88
transformation problem, the 13, 27, 64, 70, 72, 80, 81

Vaccarino, Giuseppe 25
value. *See also* commodity: commodity value
  labour theory of value 12, 13, 27, 28, 36, 47, 63, 64, 70, 75, 77, 83, 84, 88, 92

surplus value
  absolute surplus value 47, 48, 51
  relative surplus value 47, 51, 53, 56, 57, 58
value form 17, 22, 23, 24, 25, 28, 66, 91, 92
value substance 17, 23, 24, 27, 63, 71, 93
Value, Price and Profit 33, 59

wage labour 12, 16, 33, 34, 35, 38, 40, 41, 42, 43
Wolff, Richard D. 28, 81

This book need not end here...

Share

All our books — including the one you have just read — are free to access online so that students, researchers and members of the public who can't afford a printed edition will have access to the same ideas. This title will be accessed online by hundreds of readers each month across the globe: why not share the link so that someone you know is one of them?

This book and additional content is available at:
https://doi.org/10.11647/OBP.0169

Customise

Personalise your copy of this book or design new books using OBP and third-party material. Take chapters or whole books from our published list and make a special edition, a new anthology or an illuminating coursepack. Each customised edition will be produced as a paperback and a downloadable PDF.

Find out more at:
https://www.openbookpublishers.com/section/59/1

Like Open Book Publishers

Follow @OpenBookPublish

Read more at the Open Book Publishers BLOG

You may also be interested in:

Peace and Democratic Society
Edited by Amartya Sen

https://doi.org/10.11647/OBP.0014

Democracy and Power
The Delhi Lectures
Noam Chomsky. Introduction by Jean Drèze

https://doi.org/10.11647/OBP.0050

Just Managing?
What it Means for the Families of Austerity Britain
Mark O'Brien and Paul Kyprianou

https://doi.org/10.11647/OBP.0112

Tyneside Neighbourhoods
Deprivation, Social Life and Social Behaviour in One British City
Daniel Nettle

https://doi.org/10.11647/OBP.0084

www.ingramcontent.com/pod-product-compliance
Lightning Source LLC
Chambersburg PA
CBHW060032180426
43196CB00045B/2620